Diane Catchpole nee Macdonald was born in Dunfermline, Scotland, in 1941. Her mother died in 1944. Brought up by English grandparents, Diane went on a two-year family visit to Africa in 1947. She got married in 1961 and spent two years in Malta. With her second husband, she moved to Suffolk and had three children. Her writing consists of a book called Diane Who?, which is not published. She joined a friendly scribbler's group but found that the genre of fantasy was not for her—ordinary life was rich enough. And so she embarked on a voyage of discovery.

For as long as I can remember, my mum was on a quest to find out more and more about her parents, whom she never knew: her father, whom she never met, and her mother, whom, however hard she tried, she couldn't remember. Mum wanted to pass on what she had found out about her heritage to her own children so that we too could feel a connection to them. In doing this, she became a writer.

Since losing Mum this talent for writing has been an enormous comfort to us, all three of her children. Her words are now on the pages of a published book, and we are all so proud of her. If only she could have held a copy in her hands before she died, but that wasn't to be.

Your ever-loving children:

Louise (Loysidrude), Catherine (Roonie) and Ross (Smiggot and doodie doodie)

These are the people Mum wished to give thanks:

Allan Macdonald, Ray Catchpole, Carol Mackay and Rosemary Shipman.

Diane Catchpole
nee Macdonald

MACDONALD OF AIRD, MACDONALD OF THE ISLES AND A VOYAGE OF DISCOVERY

AUSTIN MACAULEY PUBLISHERS™
LONDON • CAMBRIDGE • NEW YORK • SHARJAH

Copyright © Diane Catchpole nee Macdonald 2024

The right of Diane Catchpole nee Macdonald to be identified as the author of this work has been asserted by the author in accordance with Sections 77 and 78 of the Copyright, Designs and Patents Act 1988.

All rights reserved. No part of this publication may be reproduced, stored in a retrieval system, or transmitted in any form or by any means, electronic, mechanical, photocopying, recording, or otherwise, without the prior permission of the publishers.

Any person who commits any unauthorised act in relation to this publication may be liable to criminal prosecution and civil claims for damages.

All of the events in this memoir are true to the best of author's memory. The views expressed in this memoir are solely those of the author.

A CIP catalogue record for this title is available from the British Library.

ISBN 9781035822904 (Paperback)
ISBN 9781035822911 (ePub e-book)

www.austinmacauley.com

First Published 2024
Austin Macauley Publishers Ltd®
1 Canada Square
Canary Wharf
London
E14 5AA

Table of Contents

A Journey of Discovery	11
The Birth of Madge	13
The Arrangement	18
Scotland	24
The Start of the	26
Summer Holidays	26
1926	29
Dogs	32
Family Life	38
Christmas 1933	42
The Accident	45
My Father	49
Family Matters	53
The Decision	57
The Macdonalds	58
World War II	60

The Student Nurse	61
Courtship and Marriage	65
Early Days	72
Dear Mum and Dad	81
1940	87
Scotland	91
The Train Journey	99
Home	105
The Letter…	109
India	116
The City Hospital	125
Brenda	133
Abandoned Hope	136
Epilogue	144
Home	150
Elizabeth's Wedding	154
Control	160
Macdonald Clan	173
Screams for Help	174
Suicide: The Reason Why	175
Case 1	176
Case 2	182
Case 3	188

Case 4	**200**
To Whom It May Concern	**204**
In Conclusion	**205**
Who Am I?	**206**
Finally	**208**

A Journey of Discovery

This book covers the human conditions of bonding between mother and child, parental control over children and post-traumatic stress disorder and how it can affect a person for the rest of their life.

Like many people who grew up not knowing their parents, it becomes somewhat of a life's journey to discover who they were and what kind of personality they had or anything that could explain one's own personality traits. My mother's life was in many ways tragic. Her Victorian mother never talked about her when I was growing up, something I can only attribute to guilt and the fact that grown-ups didn't discuss adult themes with children. I knew nothing of my father until I met my half-sister Liz when I was in my forties. Her welcome to me when I travelled to Canada to meet her meant a great deal.

So I begin my journey with the birth of my mother – a time to be born, a time to die. If there is such a thing, then my young mother certainly chose a particularly unfortunate time to be born. Most of the information I gleaned from stories told by family members over the years.

The strangest and most unexpected thing happened to me as this work progressed. I found a disturbing echo of my own life, something a psychiatrist could possibly explain. It seemed to me that a child raised in an excessively disciplined environment like my mother could well choose a controlling domineering partner as a lifelong companion. My own choice of life partners would go a long way to proving this theory. But that, as they say, is another story.

My mother's story gives a picture of how circumstances can affect the rest of a person's life. The fact that Madge never bonded with her mother was perhaps the reason she fell for a smooth-talking, well-educated man 20 years older than herself, who flattered her and made her feel special but carefully hid his own damaged personality.

The Birth of Madge

Lilian lay back in the marital bed cradling her tiny daughter in her arms. Gently, she traced her finger down the side of the baby's face gazing at the tiny crumpled features. She noted with satisfaction the marked resemblance to the boys, the soft strands of dark hair that clung to the baby's little round skull, the long delicate fingers that curled so trustfully round her own, the tightly closed eyes revealing long spidery eyelashes lying on the perfectly smooth cheeks. 'Yes,' Lilian smiled to herself, 'you'll do.'

The midwife sent for her husband and quickly darted about the room checking that all the telltale evidence of childbirth had been removed. It wouldn't do if "Father" were to be embarrassed by her carelessness.

Harry hurried into the room as soon as he was summoned. He went straight to Lilian's side, 'My dear, I could hear you were in a lot of pain. Is there anything wrong, or was the little devil just being awkward?'

'I think it was just the birth, but don't you think she's worth it?'

'She!' Harry was delighted; he picked up his daughter just as his two young sons ran in clamouring to see the baby. Harry stood in the doorway watching Lilian with the children gathered around, enjoying the sight of his young dominant wife for once softened by her maternal role. He adored her and had done so from the first moment they met.

Later that evening when Harry had bathed and put the boys to bed, he sat quietly talking to Lilian as she sat propped up in bed breastfeeding the baby. He noted without comment that she winced slightly when she was feeding from the right breast, whereupon the baby was shifted onto the left breast. Harry had learned very early in his marriage that too many solicitous questions led to some very abrasive responses, so wisely he kept silent.

'Well, have you decided on her name?' he asked.

'What do you think of Marjorie?' came the reply.

'Marjorie,' Harry repeated, 'yes I like that. It's a pretty name. You realise, of course, that she will probably be called Madge.'

'No, she won't,' Lilian declared stoutly, 'I detest the name Madge. If she is christened Marjorie, then Marjorie she will stay. In fact, I've decided that her full name will be Marjorie Mildred Tilla Miles. That will keep all the elderly relatives happy, including your aunt.'

The infant now fast asleep was placed back inside the bedside cot. Harry took the opportunity of putting his arm around Lilian holding her close. All of a sudden, she seemed very fragile. Glad of his strength, Lilian lay back in his arms feeling weak and not a little tearful.

Harry continued to talk quietly, 'I'll give you a hand as much as I can with the boys. Very soon, Don will go to school so that will be a help. That midwife, Mrs Jewel, isn't it? She's a bit of a tartar, isn't she? Are you sure you feel all right now?'

Harry peered down, realising suddenly that, like their little daughter, Lilian was sound asleep.

A few days later, Lilian was sitting in the chair next to her bed. She was waiting for Harry to return. He had been dispatched to register the birth of the baby at the local registrar. She heard him running up the stairs two at a time. Proudly, he came into the bedroom and presented the birth certificate to Lilian with a flourish. Lilian read the certificate with pursed lips. Her expression darkened, 'Milfred!' she exploded, 'and just who is Milfred?'

'I thought that's what you said,' Harry stammered.

'No one is called Milfred. I said MILDRED!' Lilian shouted in fury.

Harry did not reply. He found that silence was the best policy when faced with one of Lil's lightning tempers. So the baby was called Marjorie Milfred Tilla Miles, and so she remained.

Lilian sat gazing solemnly at her reflection in the bedroom mirror, her small regular features and lightly traced high cheekbones framed by abundant dark hair, which she was twisting into a sedate knot at the nape of her neck. Satisfied, at last, she rose, smoothed her dress down and went into the next room to get the children ready for the weekly shopping expedition.

Now that young Donald was at school, only Reginald and baby Marjorie needed her attention. Reg stood sentinel over his baby sister's pram wearing his smart sailor's suit. Lilian's face softened as she gently lifted Marjorie into her arms. The baby's tiny fingers curled around Lilian's finger. With her dark hair and solemn expression, she was the image of her young mother. As was the fashion of the time, the baby was dressed head to foot in pristine white. To complete the ensemble, Lilian placed a small white embroidered lace bonnet on the baby's head.

Unfortunately, Lilian hadn't picked up in health as quickly this time as after her other births. A persistent pain kept nagging in her tummy. Perhaps she should mention it to the doctor on her postnatal visit? But meanwhile, there was work to be done, shopping to be got. She manoeuvred the old black pram with its deep body and solid wheels, awkwardly through the front door.

Greta Barclay watched from behind her net curtains as young Mrs Miles negotiated her pram through the front door and down the garden path. *What a nice little respectable family*, she thought. *The little boys were polite, and their parents were friendly. It was nice to see it.* Greta watched until Lilian vanished from sight before letting the curtain fall with a little sigh. It was hard to get used to the loneliness since Les had passed on. Les had always told her off for snooping he called it, but now it had become a kind of company.

As Lilian made her way to the local shops, several people stopped to ask about her health and to admire the baby. It was a lovely bright morning, the kind that makes you glad to be alive. If it wasn't for that insistent pain, life would feel good indeed.

But, as she turned for home, the tenderness in her tummy had spread round to her back. Now it felt as if she was on fire inside. Frightened because she was in sole charge of the baby and her young son, she willed her legs to work. If she could just make it home before anything drastic happened.

Greta watched young Mrs Miles struggling up the road, turning slowly into her gateway. She watched as Lilian fumbled for her key. Then just as she inserted the key in the lock, to Greta's utter amazement, she slowly collapsed on the doorstep and laid motionless.

For Greta, it was the culmination of 30 years of snooping, the ultimate justification, the answer to a nosy neighbour's prayer, a real live drama. She flew across the road and made Lilian as comfortable as possible before she set off to the nearest telephone box to get help. For one who spent her life living vicariously through others, she really knew how to rise to a crisis. Almost sobbing with the unaccustomed effort of running, Greta managed to summon an ambulance before hurrying back to see what she could do.

Lilian was still lying motionless. As when she had left, Greta desperately wondered what she could do next and then remembered that her youngest son was due home for lunch at any moment. He could run down the dockyard and tell Harry to come home. The ancient ambulance rattled up. The last Greta saw of Lilian was of her motionless form being carried onto the stretcher and loaded into the back of the vehicle which clanged loudly and disappeared from view.

The Arrangement

Harry arrived home from his job as a dockyard policeman to find his ordered life in disarray. The baby Marjorie was wailing loudly. Reginald was still clutching the pram bewildered by the speed of events. Plans had to be made. Although Harry's boss was very sympathetic with his family problems, there was no question that he could take time off to look after the children.

Donald, of course, would go to stay with Lilian's mother in Kent. Greta was pleased enough to take young Reg under her wing, but the baby remained a problem. She was only two months old and still being breast fed.

'Do you know of anyone with a very young baby who might consider taking another one on?' Harry asked Greta anxiously.

'No, I'm afraid not,' Greta replied thoughtfully, 'but just a minute. I do know a young couple who live not too far away who might consider looking after a young baby. The wife has just started up a nursery and is looking for young children to care for. I will make enquiries if you like.'

Harry was pathetically grateful, 'I can pay, you know.'

'Yes, I expect they would want some kind of payment, and I don't expect you would like to put the baby in the workhouse, which is the only alternative,' Greta said briskly.

Harry shuddered. He could never forget that his sister Bess had been put in the workhouse when his parents died. Harry had been 10 years old at the time and his sister was two years younger. Although life with his maiden aunt hadn't been much better, Harry had always felt guilty about Bess, but he had kept in touch with her through the years and she was now happily employed in service with a sympathetic employer.

'No, no, anything but that,' Harry said spreading his hands in denial, 'besides, I don't expect Lilian will be in hospital for very long.'

'That reminds me, Mr Miles, after you have visited the hospital, could you just pop in and let me know how she is, and why she collapsed?'

As it turned out, Lilian owed her life to her nosy neighbour. She had had a very close brush with death. In fact, she was within minutes of dying from a perforated appendix when she was wheeled hastily into the operating theatre.

As she discovered much later, five other people were brought into the hospital that day suffering from peritonitis, but she was the only one to survive. One of the nurses told her that all the doctors were occupied when Lilian arrived. She was dealt with by one of the young registrars who had no practical experience and little confidence in his ability.

'Well, he must have done something right,' Lilian said with a wry smile.

But, apart from that, there was precious little to smile about. For the next six months, she hovered between life and death, her body fighting to clear itself of the dangerous infections that threatened to overwhelm her, in the days before antibiotics.

Then there was a long period of convalescence during which Lilian lay listlessly, hardly able to lift her head to acknowledge the constant presence of Harry, who was trying desperately to interest his wife in the world outside. Primarily, he talked about the children. Lilian listened as he chatted about the arrangements for the boys and how bonny Marjorie had become, but it seemed to her that he was talking about strangers. She had become totally detached. Eventually, however, it was deemed that Lilian was fit enough to return home and take up the reins of domesticity again.

Meanwhile, Lucille, the young woman who had volunteered to look after young Marjorie, realised that she had taken on a nightmare. In tears, she consulted her husband Bill, 'I just do not know what to feed the baby on. She just spits out the formula milk I bought at the co-op. I've tried cow's milk, but that was no more successful. The poor little mite is starving. She cries herself to sleep, but what on earth am I going to give her when she wakes up?'

'Don't panic love,' Bill soothed her, 'we'll take a trip to the chemist and ask for some advice there.'

The chemist pursed his lips when confronted by the problem, 'Why don't you try condensed milk? It tells you on the tin how to water it down, and you could put a little on your finger to test the baby's reaction.'

'Do you think we should try it?' Lucille said tremulously, 'I don't want to harm the little mite.'

'Can't do no harm, if it don't do no good,' was her husband's laconic reply.

So, when Marjorie woke up, she was given a finger dipped in the sweet glutinous substance just to see if she liked it. The baby latched onto the finger ravenously dispelling all doubts that this was the answer to their problems. Marjorie thrived and filled out. Complete strangers stopped to exclaim their admiration for such a bonny baby. Her cheeks filled out, her little plump arms were pinched admiringly and as she began to stand supported, her baby fat legs bowed alarmingly. The dark hair with which she was born gradually disappeared, leaving a soft peach-like fuzz all over her scalp.

Harry was delighted. Anyone could see what a good job the young couple were doing with the baby. Lilian, he was sure, would be thrilled.

The day dawned when Harry was due to bring Lilian home from the hospital. Don and Reg were already at home when the ambulance stopped outside the house and a pale shaky Lilian was led into the house leaning heavily on Harry's arm. The little boys came shyly forward to greet their mother and Lilian acknowledged them briefly before sinking into an armchair.

Harry was dispatched to collect little Marjorie. He had, of course, kept in touch regarding Marjorie's progress, but Lilian hadn't seemed interested in his reports. But, now that she felt much better, Lilian was quite excited at the thought of seeing the baby again after such a long time.

Harry came into the living room where Lilian was sitting. Triumphantly, he placed Marjorie on her mother's lap and stood back waiting for her reaction.

Lilian gazed blankly at the baby; this wasn't her baby. This enormous fair baby with bracelets of fat around her wrists and ankles; no, this couldn't be her baby. Where was her little dark cherub? Lilian searched in vain for a slight resemblance to her own child. This child was repulsive.

'What's happened to her?' Lilian appealed to Harry. 'Why is she so fat?'

'Steady on, old girl,' Harry answered. 'Lucille and Bill found that the baby didn't like dried milk because she wasn't used to it. She hadn't been weaned if you remember, but they discovered that she liked condensed milk so that was what they fed her on. So she's put on a little weight, but isn't she a bonny baby?'

Harry stroked the baby's cheek and was rewarded with a beatific smile.

'She's bald,' Lilian complained.

Harry tried to hide his concern over Lilian's surprising reaction, 'It'll grow love.'

Harry to the baby, 'Look, she has a soft cap of fluffy down on her head.'

The baby stretched her hand out towards her mother giving her a heart-breaking smile as if to ingratiate herself with this new person. Lilian drew back instinctively.

'Don't worry. She's your little Marjorie, all right!' Harry said soothingly.

'Madge,' Lilian snapped. 'Her name is Madge and I don't want to hear her called anything else.'

Harry was at a loss. He knew better than to pursue the conversation, so quietly he removed the children to see to their needs, leaving Lilian lying weakly half dozing in the chair. Perhaps given time, Lilian would come to accept the baby. Surely, it was just because she was so tired and drained after her prolonged bout in hospital. All would be well after a few days when she had had time to recover. Not for the first time, Harry underestimated his wife.

Scotland

Lilian's fourth and last child Brenda was born in 1924. Six months later, Harry was transferred from Portsmouth dockyard to Rosyth dockyard in Fife. It was not a popular move as far as the family were concerned. Lilian was appalled, in her mind *the Scots were no better than savages*.

Six-year-old Reg was devastated. He had grown very close to Greta since Lilian's illness. He spent a good deal of his time at her house. For her part, Greta was heartbroken, the little boy had become like one of her own. It was a very sad time.

So it was a very apprehensive family who boarded the train taking them to an alien environment, a point best illustrated by a conversation that took place the first time Lilian ventured out into the garden of their allotted council house. A cheerful voice hailed her, 'Hiya Hen, I'm yer new neighbour, whit dae ye think o' the hoose?'

'Mmmmmmmm,' said Lilian.

'Ah heart tell that you had fower bairns.'

'Mmmmmmmm,' said Lilian.

'Twa laddies and twa lassies. Is that no richt?'

'Mmmmmmmm,' said Lilian.

'Whaur diz yer man work, the noo?'

'Mmmmmmmm,' said Lilian.

At that point, the lady gave up and with a slight shrug of the shoulders, she went back into her house.

Her husband greeted her with a question, 'You been makin' friends wi' the neighbours?'

'Aye,' said his wife, 'but I think the pair sowel is deef.'

It was difficult for everyone to fit into their new environment. Don and Reg had to settle into their new school and within six months, Madge started school at four-and-a-half years old. On that first day, Lilian walked with Madge to her primary school. Lilian's feelings for Madge had not changed since the day that Harry had placed the little girl in her lap. She had tried to soften her attitude towards her daughter, but somehow, she could never feel the same way about her as she did about her other children.

When they arrived at the school, all the new arrivals were met in the cloakroom by the headteacher, 'Ah, Marjorie,' she said kneeling down to unbutton Madge's coat. 'I think you will find that Marjorie will fit in very quickly, Mrs Miles. She has brothers already in the school I understand? Mrs Miles?'

The headteacher stood up and turned round; of Lilian, there was no sign.

The Start of the
Summer Holidays

It was the start of the summer holidays. Seven glorious weeks stretched ahead. Aged five, Madge had just completed her first term at the local primary school. Shrieks of laughter rang around the small council garden as Reg chased Madge around in a frantic game of tag.

It was a beautiful morning, the clear Scottish air scarcely moving the laden linen line, which stretched almost the entire length of the small garden. Using the hanging sheets as camouflage, Reg managed to corner Madge and then, brushing her shoulder, he flew away shouting in triumph.

In the kitchen, Lilian had just taken a batch of buns out of the oven, laying them on a rack to cool. Full of excitement and not as careful as he might have been, Reg shot in from the garden through the kitchen door, snatching up one of the buns on the way. He was closely followed by young Madge who was still laughing, hardly aware that her mother stood behind the door motionless with narrowed eyes.

Caught up in the excitement and copying her brother, Madge too stretched out her hand to grab one of the inviting buns. With lightning speed, Lilian brought a ladle forcibly down on the back of her small daughter's hand. Madge stopped short. A stifled scream rose in the little girl's throat. Her eyes filled with involuntary tears. Lilian bent down menacingly towards the flinching child who was cradling her injured hand against her chest, 'That will teach you to steal,' Lilian hissed at Madge.

'I didn't mean to,' the little girl stuttered. 'Please, Mummy,' the child extended her uninjured hand in appeal.

Reg appeared at the hatch doorway, he had just been in time to witness his mother's venom towards his little sister. Greatly daring, Reg approached his mother, his face red with anger and fear.

'You're not fair, Mum,' he cried. 'It wasn't Madge's fault. It was mine, and I don't want the old cake anyway.' So saying, he flung the bun across the kitchen table, only to receive a clip round the ear for his pains.

'Get out of my sight, the pair of you. I've had enough of you.' Lilian spat at them.

As she advanced on her children, Reg wrapped his arm protectively around his little sister and together the children escaped hurriedly upstairs to their sanctuary.

The two children lay together on the boys' double bed, Reg holding Madge gently in his arms as she sobbed as if her heart would break. He picked up her small swollen hand and kissed it tenderly, perhaps it was possible to kiss it better.

'I'm sorry,' Madge sobbed, 'I didn't mean for you to get a beating too.'

'I don't care. Mum shouldn't have done that to you. It wasn't fair. She never hits Don like that.'

For a while the children lay quiet, apart from the catch in Madge's breath as she tried to control her sobs. Then in a sad little voice, she asked, 'Do you think Mummy hates me?'

Reg hugged his little sister, reassuringly, 'No, of course she doesn't hate you. You must never believe that, Madge. She's just got a bad temper, that's all.'

Although he spoke with confidence, Reg felt in his heart of hearts that his mother did indeed hate Madge, the reason for which was beyond him and so very unfair.

1926

The living room was a hive of industry. Seven-year-old Madge and nine-year-old Reg were together at the dining table cutting fanciful shapes out of newspaper. Don was sitting on the sofa reading a book. Two-year-old Brenda lay contentedly on the carpet studying one of her toys.

It was Madge's turn to cut the newspaper. On Reg's instructions, she cut carefully round and lifted the shape off the table. Then the dreadful deed was discovered; she had cut through the tablecloth. Madge's face blanched. The two stricken children stared at one another, appalled. Their first instinct was to try to cover up the terrible evidence because they both well knew the consequences.

Madge's eyes filled with tears as she whispered, 'I didn't mean to. Honest, I didn't mean to.'

'Shush,' Reg whispered, 'I know it was an accident; perhaps we can cover it up? I'll say it was me.'

Gratefully, Madge flashed him a tremulous smile. But it was too late. Attracted by the frantic whispering, Don walked over to the table, eyed the evidence and called out, 'Mum, come and see what Madge has done.'

Reg was furious, 'It's just like you to tell on her, Don. You really are mean.'

'Well, she would have found out anyway,' Don excused himself with a shrug.

Lilian came into the room, her eyes narrowed and her lips tightened. Without any further comment, she turned and called, 'Harry, the switch!'

Harry came into the room. He glanced at the two terrified children and turned to his furious wife, 'I really don't think we should do this, Lil.'

But Lilian was beside herself. Her fury knew no bounds.

'That was my best tablecloth and as far as I am concerned, Madge did it deliberately. She needs to learn a lesson she won't forget in a hurry. Now are you going to do it, or will I?'

'I'm so sorry, Mum. I'm sorry. I didn't mean to do it. It was an accident.' Madge pleaded.

Hoping to deflect some of Lilian's anger, Harry quickly ushered Madge out into the kitchen where he took the switch from its accustomed place beside the unit.

'For heaven's sake, Child, you know how angry your mother gets. What on earth possessed you to do such a thing?'

'Honestly, Dad, I would never do such a thing on purpose.'

'Well, it's too late now,' swishing the birch twigs through the air, Harry brought the switch lightly down on the back of Madge's legs twice. Suddenly, all hell broke loose. Lilian burst into the kitchen, snatched the switch from Harry and proceeded to rain blows down on Madge. She was followed by Reg who tried to stay her hand. In the excitement, Reg overstepped himself and hit his mother on the hand. Harry waded in between his wife and children.

'Madge, go upstairs now!' he ordered. 'And Reg, my lad, you are going to get a thrashing. Don't you dare hit your mother!'

Much later, Madge and Reg sat alone together in Reg and Don's bedroom.

'I hate Don,' Reg was incensed.

'But it was all my fault,' Madge sighed. 'Why do I do these things?'

Reg had no answer.

Dogs

The Miles family were dog lovers and most of their formative years were spent in the company of a large good-natured Airedale called Dizzy. It was Dizzy they rode on, sat on, dressed up, slept together with, romped together with and walked for miles together with. But Dizzy was essentially Harry's dog, so when Harry reported for duty at the dockyard, he often took Dizzy with him.

The large placid animal became a familiar sight to the security staff at the gate. Rabbits abounded within the dockyard complex and here, Dizzy was in his element. He grew swift and successful as a hunter. It was a rare occasion for Harry, when accompanied by Dizzy, to go out of the gates without a clutch of rabbits for Lilian to skin.

Then one day, Dizzy disappeared, simply vanished into thin air. The family were distraught. They posted notices wherever possible. The entire family combed the streets calling his name, but of the large Airedale, there was no sign.

A week after Dizzy's disappearance, Madge stood in line at the local co-op waiting patiently to collect the shopping. She was listening without interest to the conversation of the ladies in front of her.

Suddenly, one lady said, 'Did you hear about the farmer, Ian Grant. He farms that place up on Castlandhill?'

'No,' said the other woman.

'Well, last week, he apparently shot two dogs that were worrying his sheep.'

Madge's ears pricked up.

'Alsatians?' the second woman asked.

'One was; the other was one of those great big ginger-coloured dogs. I forget the name.'

Madge's heart sank; she was barely able to complete her shopping trip. She told the rest of the family when she got home and plunged the whole household into gloom. There was simply no room for error. Dizzy had been trained to kill and had merely been following his instincts, thus passed the lovable Airedale with the big heart and little judgement.

It was unthinkable to continue without a dog in the house, so Lilian hatched an idea to have pets around the place and perhaps make a little money into the bargain. She decided to breed Cairn terriers. The garden in their three-roomed terrace house was too small to accommodate the dogs. So Lilian leased a couple of old sheds about half a mile from the house and Harry converted them into kennels. It wasn't ideal, but provided the family pulled together, it was possible.

Of course, pulling together meant that a lot of the feeding and walking fell to the children. In the summer it was a pleasure, but volunteers were harder to find in winter.

'Do you think it would be too much for me to ask you to feed the dogs today?' Lilian's heavy sarcasm grated on Madge's nerves.

The first fall of winter snow came a few days after Christmas. It was bitterly cold with a biting east wind.

'Of course not, Mum. I'll get the stuff ready,' Madge said quickly.

'I'll come with you,' Brenda offered. Madge smiled at her in gratitude.

The two girls walked briskly up to the top of the steep windy hill between Rosyth and Inverkeithing, where they stood breathlessly leaning against the five-bar gate that was home to Lilian's eight Cairn terriers, their breath coming in clouds of white steam. Both Madge and Brenda dreaded this visit, Madge especially as she was given the task of looking after Brenda and making sure that she came to no harm.

However, the task of feeding the dogs had a further hazard in the shape of a huge goose called Delicious, a name that owed more to his culinary prospects than to his nature. In fact, as Madge swung the gate open, a warning hiss greeted her. A large goose with wings and neck at full stretch came flying out from behind the kennels with his razor-sharp beak ready to snap at any intruders, to cause untold damage.

'Delicious!' Madge cried in welcome.

The goose stopped short as his old eyes recognised a friend. Checking himself abruptly, he ruffled his feathers and muttering like an old man, stalked off with dignity intact.

Madge smiled at this incident. She remembered a previous occasion when Delicious was much younger and the girls had been dispatched to feed the dogs when they got back from school. By the time, they had changed out of their school uniform and got loaded up, darkness was beginning to fall. By the time, they reached the five-bar gate, it was pitch dark. Brenda, nervous of the dark, hung back leaving Madge to swing open the heavy gate and enter the small yard.

Suddenly, a loud hiss made her jump. Too late she remembered the guard goose, not visible but plainly audible; he came rushing out of his corner to repel all boarders. It was too late for the advance and be recognised technique; besides, it was too dark. Madge made a sharp exit via the top of the entrance gate. Tactics were discussed in a whisper as the two girls decide how best to approach the problem.

It is perhaps worth noting that it never occurred to either of them to just give up and go home. Such was Lilian's influence even in absence. Madge eventually hit upon a brilliant wheeze relying on a diversionary ploy. Brenda had to swing into the yard clinging onto the gate and rattling the chain links that held the padlock in place, while Madge slipped over to the kennels and joined the dogs. After the dogs were fed, Madge would shout to Brenda who would repeat the procedure again to allow Madge time to regain the safety of the gate.

It all went like a well-rehearsed routine. Brenda acted as a very credible decoy, while Madge carried out the task. It would have worked too but for the fact that the hem of Madge's dress snagged on a nail as she flew out of the kennel heading for the gate. She was caught in the path of a furious goose flying towards her, neck outstretched, squawking stridently and intent on taking a sizeable chunk out of her anatomy. Then, with an ominous ripping sound, the dress parted company with the nail and Madge was free to scramble for the gate scraping and bumping her knees as she went, closely followed by a snapping beak.

The two little girls landed in a heap in the lane, at first relieved at their narrow escape, then with consternation at the sight of Madge's ruined dress. What on earth was she going to tell her mother? Brenda put her hands over her mouth and her eyes filled with horror.

'Don't tell Mum, Madge. Please don't tell Mum. You'll only get a beating from Dad. You know you will. I hate it when you get hit. I just hate it.' Brenda stamped her feet and burst into tears.

Madge put her arms around her little sister and held her close, 'You mustn't get so upset, lovely. I have to tell Mum. It would be much worse when she finds out later. Besides, the beating looks worse than it is. Dad just does it to please Mum. He doesn't hit as hard as he could, honest.'

This story of the kennels has a rather sad sequel. A couple of years later, Lilian made the decision to give up her breeding programme. She kept two of her favourites and sold her remaining dogs. The implications of this move were lost on the children, until Christmas Day that is. Triumphantly, Lilian came into the room bearing a large platter on which rested an enormous roast goose.

'That's Delicious!' Reg crowed.

Madge and Brenda froze, watching in horror as Harry carved slices off and laid them on their plates. The situation was desperate for the girls: The unfailing rule in the Miles' household embodied the maxim that anything served on the plate had to be eaten regardless of personal taste or preference. Brenda's eyes filled with tears and she pleaded to get down from the table. Lilian was perfectly aware of Madge and Brenda's distress and the reason for it, but it occasioned only exasperation on her part.

'Eat it up!' Lilian snapped at Madge, but Madge put her hands over her mouth to disguise an involuntary heave.

Lilian's temper flared, 'Get out of my sight, the pair of you. I don't want to see you again today and there's no dinner for either of you!'

Thankfully, the girls fled the scene, aware that it could have been much worse. So their Christmas Day was spent in their bedroom.

Family Life

Lilian was harassed; the children wisely kept quiet and out of her way as much as possible. The reason wasn't hard to discover. Lilian and Harry were going on holiday. They were going for a week; provisions had to be garnered, lists made, clothes washed and cases packed. Finally, the day arrived. Lilian and Harry left in a flurry of instructions for the four children they were leaving behind.

'Don, you are in charge.' Don flashed a triumphant smile at his siblings.

'Reg, you behave yourself and do as you are told. If you don't I'll hear about it, don't you worry.'

'Madge, you can do the cooking.'

'Brenda, you do what Don tells you.'

With that, the door closed and the children were left alone. Don was 16, Reg was 14, Madge was 12 and Brenda was 8 years old. For the first time in their lives, the children were free to help themselves from the kitchen pantry, no one to scold them, no punishments to be meted out.

The opportunity was too much to resist. Within the hour, the boys had eaten most of the food that didn't need to be cooked. Madge had no idea how to cook a family meal. Besides, Lilian kept a fairly frugal cupboard, so for the next few days, the children lived mainly on bread and potatoes. Brenda spent a lot of the week in tears, 'I'm hungry, Madge. I'm hungry.'

Madge was cross with the boys for eating all the food in the beginning, but now the main concern was simply to try and keep body and soul together. Four hungry children were delighted when the day came for their parents to return. The last thing left in the cupboard was a very old stale, slightly green loaf of bread.

Madge had heard somewhere that if you wet a loaf of bread, then popped it in the oven; it would come out crisp and rejuvenated. So she dunked the loaf vigorously in the basin and put it in the oven. If it hadn't been so serious, it might have been comical to see the anticipation on the four young faces waiting to see a lovely golden loaf emerge. Their utter dismay as a large, unpleasant, steaming pile of grey inedible stodge was revealed.

The young sisters were very close and spent many happy hours together in their bedroom. At one of these sessions, the girls were giggling about the total discomfiture and embarrassment of their brothers. It was not very often that such an opportunity arose, so they were making the most of it.

The reason for their hilarity involved their mother's sewing skills. Lilian had made many attempts over the years to perfect her dressmaking ability, but the trouser zips on the boys' school uniform defeated her. Compromise was the order of the day and what she eventually produced was a kind of vertical letter box in the front of their trousers pulled together with snap fasteners. The girls thought it was priceless, and so no doubt did the boys' schoolmates.

Not long after the holiday debacle, Madge and Brenda were sitting in their bedroom chatting; unlike many older sisters, Madge had no qualms about sharing confidences with her little sister. Brenda was laying across the bed her legs kicking lazily in the air. Madge was sitting on the iron bedstead swinging idly as she chatted to Brenda.

Suddenly, Madge's foot slipped and she swung completely round and thumped her head very hard on the iron underside of the bed. With a muffled grunt of agony, she collapsed on the floor. Brenda was frightened by Madge's white face and rapidly swelling forehead, 'I'll go and tell Mum,' the little girl said with concern.

Madge felt sick and dizzy but when Brenda's words penetrated her mind, she pleaded, 'No, please, don't Brenda. Mum has told me off before for swinging on the bed. She'll kill me if she finds out. Please don't, lovey.'

'But you've got a huge lump on your forehead. She's bound to see it. You know what she's like.' Brenda was close to tears.

'Not if you help me,' Madge pleaded.

'How?' Brenda asked.

'What if I part my hair over this way? What do you think?'

'I can still see it poking out. It looks as if it is going black.'

'How about this then?' Madge asked.

'That's better,' said Brenda.

'Dinner!' shouted Lilian.

'Coming!' Madge and Brenda replied in unison.

Christmas 1933

Roars of laughter and hoots of derision greeted Lilian as she pushed open the living room door. The whole family was at home. The house was buzzing with excitement. This was to be the last time that all of her children would be gathered together for the Christmas festival, although of course Lilian did not know this at the time.

Reg was holding up one of Madge's Christmas presents, a pair of black lace French knickers, and cavorting around the room.

'I say, I say, aren't these a fetching pair? Just my colour too.'

Madge snatched the knickers back, saying in mock exasperation, 'Goodness sake, Reg, grow up!'

Lilian's eyes traversed the room resting fondly on her eldest and favourite son Don, who had recently begun his course at Edinburgh studying medicine; as usual, he was sitting apart from his brother and sisters, his head deep in a book. He had grown into a tall dark and classically handsome young man, but he was in turn taciturn and irritable.

'For goodness sake, Reg, pipe down, will you?' he growled.

The two brothers had never managed to get along together in harmony. If they were together for any length of time, sparks were bound to fly. Subsiding onto the sofa, Reg grinned. Smaller and slighter than his older brother, his fine dark hair flopping over his eyes – incidentally, a source of great irritation to his mother. Somehow, he never seemed to get his hair cut as short as Lilian thought he should.

Madge caught her mother's eye as she went to sit beside Reg on the sofa. *Funny, how those two hung together. It must be something to do with being in the middle of the family*, Lilian thought.

Her eyes narrowed as she watched her first-born daughter surreptitiously. If it was possible to dislike one of one's own children, then it was true to say that Lilian disliked Madge, even the fact that the girl was shy was a matter for exasperation. In any family disputes, Madge invariably got the blame; there weren't many things Madge got right. Reg and Brenda tried to defend their sister whenever they could, but they couldn't be around all of the time. Lilian was aware of the reason for her dislike, but she was unable to either control or prevent her feelings.

Madge, on the other hand, was vaguely puzzled by the strength of her mother's antipathy, but being a cheerful optimistic girl on the whole, she had long accepted the situation. She just shrugged and tried to keep out of her mother's way as much as possible.

Moving from her eldest daughter with an inaudible sigh, Lilian's eyes softened as she looked at her youngest child. Brenda was busy writing in her new diary. Her thick very dark hair shaped into the latest bob, her face solemn in concentration. Just then the door opened and Harry came into the room. He settled himself into the only vacant chair in the room, vacant only because it was "Dad's chair" and therefore sacrosanct. Only Brenda dared to sit in it and she was always turfed out with a grin.

Lilian told her assembled family of the brilliant idea for cooking the turkey that year, 'I'm sick of the turkey being cooked in too much fat, so I have hung the bird up by the legs so that the fat can drip off. While still cooking the bird, all the fat will be left in the tray at the bottom of the oven.'

Beaming she looked round for approval and all the heads nodded in unison.

'Seems like a good idea, Mum,' Reg said.

The talk moved to more general topics: politics, education and soon a lively discussion ensued during which Don moved over to play his newly acquired classical record *The Poet and Peasant*. Almost immediately, Reg got up and changed the record to the popular Allan Jones hit, *The Donkey Serenade*.

'I think there will be another world war breaking out here in a minute.' Madge remarked as Don's face went white with rage as he rushed over to the record player to change it back.

'I say, old man,' Reg began, but whatever Reg was about to say was lost as from the kitchen came a loud ominous muffled thump.

The entire family rose as one and rushed out to investigate the noise. Lilian opened the oven door. For a moment, everyone was stunned into silence by the sight of a large turkey lying in a pan of well-spattered grease, with a pair of thoroughly cooked turkey legs suspended from the top shelf. The comical sight of dismay on Lilian's face sent everyone off into loud gusts of hysterical laughter.

The Accident

Sometime after dinner, Madge sat quietly in her shared bedroom doing her homework when her bedroom door opened abruptly and Reg slipped in. He closed the door quietly and stood with his back to it, his breath coming in ragged gulps as if he had been running.

Madge knew that he had come home unexpectedly. He was six weeks into his RAF pilot training and was not expected to have any home leave for quite a few months. She had no idea what circumstances had brought him home. He had been closeted in the living room with their parents for at least an hour. Voices raised in anger had floated up causing Madge to wrinkle her brow in puzzlement, wondering what on earth Reg had done to deserve such hostility.

Instinctively, feeling that Reg needed sympathy, not questions, Madge rose and went to sit down on the bed, patting the quilt, indicating that he could come and sit beside her. Reg's stricken white face frightened her. He sat down wordlessly, dropping his face into his hands. Silently, they sat together until the shadows of the setting sun sent her long fingers into the little room.

With his face still hidden, slowly, Reg began to talk. In a low monotone, he poured out the sorry tale of how his dreams had vanished and his world had collapsed, to the only listener who would truly understand.

The only thing that Reg had ever wanted to do was join the RAF as a pilot officer, an ambition that was realised when he was accepted by the recruitment board as a trainee pilot. He was young, impetuous and enthusiastic. The Air Force beckoned with the promise of unlimited adventure. Each day underlined what a good choice he had made; he managed the theoretical work with effortless ease and he was the best young pilot on his course. But it was in the air that he really came into his own. He proved to be a quick and able pupil. His reflexes were like lightning and his handling of the small training aircraft inspired confidence in the world-weary training officer lumbered with the daunting task of providing the country with as many young pilots as possible, as quickly as possible, as the rumours of war escalated.

This same officer was standing near the Conning tower following the first solo flights of his young trainees with a pair of powerful field binoculars when suddenly into his field of view came the distinctive shape of a tiger moth. It was the antics of the pilot that held the interest of the older man as he swept the skies keeping the small aircraft in sight.

'Crazy young bugger,' he muttered, as he watched Reg wheeling and swooping, climbing and diving, showing off as only an exuberant young man, supremely confident in his own ability, dares to do.

But then disaster struck as Reg clipped the topmost branch of a very tall tree, destabilising the small aircraft. Fighting to keep an even keel, he was forced to put the plane down in an adjacent field to the airstrip. The uneven ground tore the wheels off, extensively damaging the fragile undercarriage.

As it ground to a halt, part of the nearside wing snapped off and the aircraft slewed onto its side.

White and shaken Reg sat tightly gripping the steering column. Loud voices and hands tapping on the side of the aircraft brought him to his senses. Slowly, he climbed out. One of the ground crew members patted him sympathetically on the arm, 'Are you all right, old chap?'

When Reg nodded, he went on, 'I say, old man, that was dashed bad luck! Crikey, here comes the big brass.'

Reg looked up to see the station commander advancing with a thunderous expression on his face. The next few minutes were some of the most unpleasant ever faced by the young man. The upshot being that Reg was summarily dismissed from the service. It was a scene that was repeated when he had to face his parents to explain what happened.

Lilian was particularly incensed by her younger son's reckless behaviour and she used this opportunity to reinforce the difference between her two sons, to Reg's detriment of course.

When Reg finally stopped talking, he turned his stricken face to his young sister and said despairingly, 'What on earth am I going to do now, Madge?'

Before she had time to reply, the tension of having to keep an expressionless front in the face of unrestrained anger from the station commander coupled with the antagonism faced at home, Reg's face crumpled. He put his head in his sister's lap and wept like a broken-hearted child. Madge sat motionless, stroking her brother's hair gently. When he regained his composure, she listened sympathetically as Reg poured out his frustration and disappointment in a muted whisper lasting well into the evening.

When he had talked himself to a standstill, Madge did her best to rally his spirits. It wasn't the end of the world. She assured him that he could still join the RAF and pilots weren't the only people needed. Finally, Reg left to go to his own bedroom. The seeds of hope and encouragement sown by his younger sister already starting to take root.

My Father

Alastair Reginald Macdonald was born on 6 January 1899 to an influential family of Scottish heritage. His father Reginald James Macdonald was a Colonel in the Royal Artillery and a gifted military artist. The boy Alastair grew up in England living mainly in Surrey with his grandmother, as his mother and father had a highly social life.

I know that my father left Wellington College in 1917 when he was 18 years old. He was a typical privileged public schoolboy; confident, clever, looking forward to starting a successful life, beginning with a posting to his father's regiment the Royal Horse Artillery during the First World War.

Rex's first assignment was as a subaltern in the Royal Horse Artillery, for which he later received the following reference: *He had entire charge of some 40 horses, these he took over in indifferent condition and being cared for by a difficult lot of men. He put in some very excellent work and proved his capacity for running men and looking after horses by making a very marked improvement in his command in a short time under winter conditions on active service—a high test of horsemanship.*

Rex's next assignment was with the School of Gunnery in Shoeburyness. His reference went as follows: *He had sole charge of 50 or 60 horses as well as their appointments and harness. Not only did he prove himself to be a most capable horse master, but he also showed great tact, firmness and ability in the handling and command of men. I had implicit confidence in him and recommend him for appointment to the Royal Horse Artillery. He was a conscientious worker, smart and willing to turn his hand to anything.*

Rex's last reference before joining the troops in the French trenches is listed: *He is keen and energetic and is a very good soldier by birth and tradition. He is very good with men and will make a really good officer. He has good manners and is a nice clean-looking smart fellow and is the type we want as officers. I very strongly recommend that this officer be given every chance of obtaining a regular commission.*

I think these references paint a good picture of the kind of young man my father was. Before the war, horses were his love. He had been brought up with them, so in many ways he was a natural for the Royal Horse Artillery. Rex joined his regiment entrenched in the front lines fighting the third battle of Ypres, known to history as the Battle of Passchendaele. Although regarded as a victory, a lot of soldiers lost their lives until Passchendaele fell to the Canadian troops on 10 November 1917.

The guns had fallen silent. The sky darkened and rain began to fall as it had done continually for most of the previous months of August and September. The trench was full of dirty muddy water through which the troops sloshed, unable to avoid the constant downpour. Two young soldiers sat together in the trench; their feet planted in the water, huddling under waterproof capes, covering their filthy uniforms.

It was a brief moment of respite supplied by the field kitchens in the form of sandwiches wrapped in paper bags. Rex, for he was one of the boys, hadn't been posted to the front for very long before he found a good friend, a young soldier of a similar age. Together the young lads sat eating the sandwiches provided, relaxing, chatting and laughing despite the horrendous surroundings. Neither of them heard the approaching stray shell. It entered the trench and landed squarely on the head of Rex's young friend, tearing down his body until the young man was literally cut in half. Rex was liberally sprayed with his blood.

For Rex, time stood still. An older soldier alerted by the thump of the shell came running up.

'Christ Almighty!' he said and turning, shouted at the top of his voice for help.

As soldiers came running from all over the trench, he turned back to Rex and asked, 'Are you all right?'

Rex sat frozen, his eyes staring sightlessly ahead. Slowly, he turned his head and looked at the mangled remains of his companion. Then silently he keeled over and fell into the water-filled trench. After being hauled out of the putrid water, Rex was sent to a support trench where a medic, realising Rex was suffering badly from shock, ordered his withdrawal to Base Camp where he was cleaned up before reporting back for duty.

Recently, I have been hearing about post-traumatic stress disorder, a condition now recognised as psychological trauma brought on by a patient experiencing a terrifying situation over which they have no control. The point I would like to make is that this situation, as well as being terrifying at the time, can affect a person for the rest of their life.

I have no doubt that many thousands, hundreds of thousands in fact, came home from the bloodbath that was World War I, suffering symptoms similar to my father's. Perhaps that contributed to the feelings of many that it was the lucky ones who were killed. Having read about PTSD, I realise that my father, due to his experience in World War I, ticks most of the boxes.

Family Matters

Nothing more is known about Rex's military career, except that he was given a Commission in the Royal Horse Artillery on 4 November 1917, a week before the Battle of Passchendaele was won. I think that Rex left France, when the war ended, a changed man. Possibly that made him decide to relinquish his Commission in the Royal Horse Artillery on 20 September 1920.

Now Rex was forced to think about what he was going to do in civvy street. His thoughts drifted to his estranged parents, but as he had gone straight into the Royal Horse Artillery from Wellington College, he didn't really feel that he fitted into their lives anymore. His relationship with his parents had always been difficult. His father was a Colonel DSO in the Royal Artillery and he was likely to ask some very awkward questions. So that was not to be a consideration.

So Rex turned to his grandmother as he had many times in the past. She lived in Chobham in Surrey and she loved her grandson unconditionally, so much so that she had settled a trust fund on him for life.

Rex's grandmother couldn't believe her eyes. There, standing on the doorstep was her beloved boy. She was absolutely delighted. Later as they sat together in front of a cosy fire, Rex told his grandmother that he was short of money except for his army severance pay but was reluctant to go home to his parents and had no idea how to proceed with his life. His grandmother took his hands in hers and pressed them to her chest, 'Don't think any more about it, my love. You are welcome to anything I can give you.'

'How can I ever repay you, Nan?' he said.

His grandmother provided all his meals and funded him to set up stables and to pursue all the things that interested him; racing bikes, cars, indulging his passion for riding horses. Life was good, but it got even better when the old lady paid for a flat in Jermyn Street, Mayfair. Rex now mingled with high society and eventually met a beautiful model called Sylvia Craske, who modelled for Selfridges.

They married within a year in 1925 and in 1926, their daughter Elizabeth was born. The only cloud on the horizon was Rex's inability to sleep without nightmares despite drinking copious quantities of alcohol in the nearest public house. It slowly began to dawn on Sylvia that Rex was unlikely to make either a good husband or a reliable father to their young daughter Elizabeth. He seemed incapable of considering others, almost as if there was something missing in his personality.

When Elizabeth was three years old, Rex and Sylvia parted. It appears that Sylvia ran off with one of the grooms employed by Rex, leaving her young daughter with her father, who hastily passed her on to his 84-year-old grandmother. Elizabeth never saw her mother again.

The reason was that divorce law at the time stated that custody of any children was given to the "innocent" party, regardless of any custodial difficulties the family might have.

Also, a married couple must have been married for seven years before divorce proceedings could take place.

So the first life that Rex had a hand in shaping was Elizabeth (known as Liz). It's ironic that although he had overall custody, he actually had very little to do with her upbringing. Liz's first memory was being taken away from her father in a big black car, in the company of an old lady who was in charge of everything. She turned out to be Liz's great-grandmother. Although the old lady loved her grandson, unfortunately, her loving feelings did not extend to his daughter.

To Liz, her great-grandmother became known as Grannie Ogre. She was domineering, eccentric, manipulative and cruel in many ways. Her punishments were Victorian and designed to fit the crime. If Liz wet the bed, she was made to sleep in an old tin bath. If she danced in front of the mirror, the mirrors were covered lest she succumbed to vanity. If Liz cried and she often did, it was called a tantrum and she was dunked in a bath of cold water. At Christmas time, presents were placed on top of the wardrobe in plain sight to encourage self-control.

After some time, an elderly niece in her sixties asked to join the household when she was widowed. Liz did not remember much about her father during these years. She remembers him dropping in and living on and off with their peculiar household. He stayed in bed a lot, and there were quite a few verbal arguments, which was, the child supposed, to do with his drinking.

One eventful day arrived, Liz was sobbing over one of Grannie Ogre's punishments. Rex gathered the desolate child into his arms, and in a rare moment of guilt, decided to take the child away from his grandmother. Sitting her on the back of his bicycle, they set off up the lane. The trip was doomed however; before they reached the end of the lane Liz fell off and Rex was forced to return the child to her erstwhile home.

Eventually, Grannie Ogre fell ill both mentally and physically, and at 89, she became unfit to look after Liz. A decision had to be made.

The Decision

The Macdonald family gathered together in Rex's sister Mary's living room: Mary, her Brigadier husband Kenneth, Rex's parents Reginald and Maye, Rex, Elizabeth and Mary's two daughters, Maryjean and Caroline. The subject under discussion was the future of Elizabeth. Rex sat helplessly, shrugging his shoulders.

Mary, his sister, took charge of the discussion by saying categorically that taking Elizabeth into her family was totally out of the question. They had two girls of their own, and they had to take priority. Ken's head nodded in agreement. Rex's eyes moved to his mother and father in appeal.

'Well,' his mother said, 'we are thinking of staying in a hotel in Nairn. Elizabeth could stay with us, but we would need help when required.'

'Fixed then,' Mary said briskly. 'Make us a cup of tea Kenneth. Sit up Maryjean, don't slouch.'

The Macdonalds

A new stage in Liz's life began. She felt afraid of these strange relations. Although her grandparents were very kind, they had no idea what to do with an eight-year-old girl. Liz was told she was very timid and wary of people and didn't like to be hugged, so the answer lay in a boarding school.

Liz was still wetting the bed apparently, but fortunately the school matron was very understanding. This time Liz was lucky. The chosen boarding school was interested in the theatrical arts, something that chimed with Liz's interests. I remember Liz telling me that her grandparents did indeed take to living in a hotel in Nairn. They managed by renting a room adjacent to the hotel so that they could monitor Liz's movements.

Liz rarely saw her father during this time in her life. Once he arrived to take her out in the school holidays thinking that if he introduced his young daughter to his horses, then she might develop an interest in them, but it proved to be a miserable failure because to the child the horse had huge brown teeth that frightened her.

Eventually, in 1937, when Liz was around 10 years old, her grandparents took an elegant flat in London. Liz many years later told me about the day her father arrived and took her out to lunch. He took her to a very posh restaurant, and then, as soon as they were seated, spotted an old acquaintance at the bar. Rex promptly left Liz at the table, joined his friend and left his young daughter sitting all alone for two hours.

The next few years for Liz were a lottery. She was passed around the Macdonald family to whoever would have her during the school holidays. A particular relative who made no secret of the fact that she was resentful of the imposition of her niece was Mary Garner Smith, Rex's younger sister. Mary had two daughters of her own, and her husband Kenneth was C in C of Fort George. No one was more aware of her importance in Scottish society than Mary. Snobbish to a fault, she didn't think that Liz fitted into her society role. More of Liz later.

World War II

Rex felt his life slipping away. His grandmother, the mainstay of his existence, had passed away. He sold his house and his horses, but somehow, he found it impossible to get organised and find a decent job. Meanwhile, World War II had begun. It meant the country had come alive, people were rushing hither and thither and Army, Navy and Airforce uniforms filled the London Streets.

Suddenly, Rex had a flash of inspiration, the Royal Horse Artillery, what on earth was he waiting for? He fetched up at the Recruitment Office on 16 November 1939 and signed the enlistment paper as a riding master. So, at the start of his new army career, Rex was posted to guarding a local waterworks and he found a bedsit in the centre of London.

The Student Nurse

When Madge first left her grammar school with a couple of "Highers", she knew without a doubt that she wanted to be a nurse. So, after a year working in a home for the elderly, she made her decision. The result of which saw Madge and her father waiting on the platform for the train that would take her away from home for the first time, to a new life and a nursing career in St George's Hospital, London.

Awkwardly, Harry held Madge in his arms. He was sorry she was going but curiously relieved that he wouldn't have to witness the unfair confrontation between his wife and his daughter anymore.

'Bye, Dad,' Madge tried to keep the catch out of her voice.

Swiftly, the train bore her away from all she had ever known, and a great adventure beckoned. It was late in the day when Madge arrived at the nurses' home, a large grey ugly building attached to the main hospital. She was greeted by a stern-faced member of staff and escorted to a room on the first floor.

A pretty girl with short dark hair answered the sharp knock. She held out her hand to greet Madge, her face wreathed in smiles, 'You must be Marjorie Miles. I'm glad to meet you. I'm Rosie Dereham.'

Rosie had apparently arrived a couple of days before Madge so she knew the general layout of the home. She was also able to give Madge some invaluable advice, 'Never leave any personal stuff lying around especially stockings or make-up. Always lock them up in your suitcase and carry the key about with you wherever you go.'

When Madge questioned this, Rosie said solemnly, 'The girls round here are thieves. I really mean that. They'll grab anything that isn't nailed down. I've lost a few things myself so I know what I am talking about.'

So, with Rosie's help, Madge soon settled into the routine. The young would-be nurses had practical studies on the wards to do as well as attending group studies and lectures with a fair amount of homework to do in the evenings. It was a busy life and left little time to socialise. Talk was all of the war and the certainty that it would be all over in a matter of months. Madge wrote home regularly, but she never received any response.

Christmas 1939 approached and everyone agreed that it would be good to get the prelims out of the way in order to have a carefree Christmas. Madge had already decided not to go home for Christmas. Money was tight, and Rosie was staying put too. On Christmas Eve, all the young nurses donned their uniforms and the hospital lights were dimmed. Together, they walked from ward to ward with lighted lanterns singing all the traditional carols. It was an uplifting sight for all those patients lucky enough to see it.

One such patient was Alastair Macdonald, a short-stay patient in the hospital for a minor operation. He looked at the fresh young faces singing their hearts out and felt incredibly moved. Then he saw her. Madge was in the centre of the choir.

She was concentrating on holding the tune when she became aware that someone was watching her. His gaze was so intense, Madge coloured up and stepped out of sight behind one of her companions as the choir moved on.

Two days later, Madge was standing in a queue in the hospital canteen when a hand fell lightly on her shoulder, 'I'm the chap you saw when you were with your carol singers. May I introduce myself?'

Madge turned and saw an older man of medium height with brown hair, blue eyes and no particular distinguishing features.

'My name is Alastair Macdonald, but I'm usually known as Rex. I'm in the army, Honourable Artillery actually. I'm quite harmless and I would very much appreciate it if you would join me for a drink on New Year's Eve.'

Instinctively, Madge wanted to refuse his polite request. She tried to think of a good excuse on the spur of the moment, without causing offence.

'It's very kind of you to offer but…'

Rex raised his hand, 'Before you crush me completely, I promise to bring my credentials if I can see you again…please? The nearest pub is the King's Head, just outside the gates of the nurses' home. I'll be there at 7 o'clock on the dot.'

'Well, I won't promise anything,' Madge said cautiously.

'You're an angel,' said Rex.

Right up until the time Rex had arranged, Madge had no intention of taking up his offer of a drink, but somehow when the time came and against Rosie's best advice, Madge found herself pushing open the door of the King's Head and going into the crowded smoky atmosphere. At first, Madge could not pick Rex out, but a tall man in a smart army uniform approached her, 'My angel has arrived,' he said.

Madge was startled, Rex had undergone an amazing transformation.

He led her to a nearby table, where they sat together and completed their introductions. Rex had an astonishing tale to tell his young listener. He admitted that he was 39. He also told her that he was a Highlander and that his family home was in Inverness where his Colonel father and mother still lived.

He was in fact a Macdonald of the Isles, an important highland family with a long proud history. He had been married a long time ago and had a child, a daughter called Elizabeth, who was at boarding school. He had owned riding stables in his youth and in fact, he was a riding master in the army. He loved horses and admitted that they were a large part of his life.

Madge was enthralled, to a young impressionable girl like her it all sounded very romantic. It seemed that in no time at all, the landlord was calling for a countdown to midnight.

On the stroke of midnight, Rex kissed Madge chastely on the cheek, then made arrangements to pick her up from the nurses' home in a couple of days. Later, Madge told Rosie all about her date. Rosie was rather dubious, 'He's a little bit too old for you, isn't he, Madge?'

'But he's a perfect gentleman, Rosie, and he comes from such an amazing family.'

Courtship and Marriage

Both Rosie and Madge passed their prelims effortlessly, after which they were allocated their respective wards. Rex and Madge continued to meet and enjoy each other's company. Sometimes, they would go for a drink, sometimes for a walk, sometimes to the cinema and occasionally for a meal. Although they both worked shifts, it was possible to meet at least three or four times a week.

Madge remained in thrall to this sophisticated man who was full of amazing stories, who treated her like a Queen; she had never felt so cherished. It was all too good to be true, at least that is how Rosie saw it. She was not so easily convinced but Madge wasn't willing to listen.

One evening, when the couple had been going out together for about five months, they were sitting in one of London's pretty parks in the late spring sunshine. Rex suddenly fell on his knees, took Madge's hand in his and asked her to marry him. For a moment, Madge was nonplussed, but then the romance of it all overwhelmed her.

'Oh, Rex, I would love to marry you.'

Kissing her hand, Rex murmured again and again, 'Thank you, thank you, oh my love, thank you.'

'I will have to let my mum and dad know of course,' Madge said after she had had time to digest the exciting news.

'Ah,' said Rex, 'I am looking forward to seeing them as soon as possible, so I think we should just make it a lovely surprise.'

'Do you think so?' said Madge doubtfully.

'Without a doubt,' said Rex.

Not long after this conversation, Rex informed Madge that he had managed to get a bedsitter in the Thames Ditton area.

'The place is no great shakes, but the area is lovely and it'll be handy for the hospital and the waterworks.' He told her, 'I'd like you to come and see the place if you don't mind.'

Madge's face lit up, 'I'd love to.'

As they alighted from the taxi, Madge looked at the tall three-storey Victorian building.

'We're at the top I'm afraid,' Rex apologised.

'Lovely,' Madge clapped her hands, 'should be a lovely view.'

As they walked up the creaking wooden stairs, a buxom lady in a pinafore came out of the ground flat.

She called, 'Coooeee!'

Rex turned round and introduced Madge to their landlady, Mrs Jenkins. Madge sensed that there were a million things that this inquisitive woman wanted to ask her, not least about the disparity in ages between Rex and herself, but thankfully, after initial introductions, Rex firmly turned his back and continued to mount the stairs.

As they walked into the large high-ceilinged room, Madge felt a slight feeling of disappointment. However, anxious not to convey her feelings to Rex and give possible offence, she exclaimed enthusiastically, 'It's lovely, Rex. We'll soon make it homely.'

Moving swiftly over to the window, she glanced out. The street below was full of traffic, but as the buildings on the other side of the street were of the same height as the building she was in, very little of the view she had hoped for was visible.

'Never mind, my angel. This is only a temporary situation. When I make Captain, we'll be able to move into a proper place.'

Rex put his arms around his bride-to-be. Madge felt so safe and loved; what did it matter about their surroundings?

So it was that six months after that fateful meeting in the King's Head on 6 June 1940, Madge and Rex got married in the local registry office, a couple of Rex's army buddies and Rosie acting as witnesses. After the ceremony, they all went back to the bedsit that Rex had acquired in Thames Ditton to celebrate the happy event.

Madge had seen Rex drink on many social occasions and it never seemed to have the slightest effect on him. But this time, it was different. Drink flowed freely all afternoon and on into the evening, the men getting drunker and louder with every passing hour.

Rosie rose to leave after a few drinks. Pressing Madge's hand anxiously, she whispered, 'I think you had better get rid of those two rotters at fast as you can.'

The three men tried hard to get Madge to join them in a drink, but when she politely refused stating that she was, in fact, teetotal, they shrugged and lost interest. From then on, she ceased to exist for them. At midnight, Madge retired behind the makeshift curtain screening the bed from the rest of the room, hurt and bewildered that Rex should prefer to drink with his friends rather than spend his honeymoon night with his new wife.

It was at least a couple of hours before the "lads" left and Rex staggered in. He passed out on the bed beside her. His face slack and with mouth agape, he began to snore stertorously.

The next day, it was well past noon before Rex arose, he was quiet and uncommunicative. Madge waited in vain for an apology, a sign even of regret, but she was doomed to disappointment. They passed the day quietly. Madge tried out her cooking skills, honed by Lilian to a fair degree of proficiency. After tea, Madge was aghast when Rex suggested that they go down to the local pub and have a few pints, 'But I don't want to go, Rex. I don't really enjoy it and I thought that now we're married…'

'Exactly,' Rex snapped, 'now we're married, you'll go where I go and like it, my lady. Besides, my friends will be waiting for me and I'm not going to let them down.'

What about letting me down? Madge thought mutinously, but wisely kept her own counsel.

The pub was full when they arrived. Thick choking smoke wreathed around the crowded room. The walls and ceiling were covered in yellowish-brown nicotine stains, the legacy of years of smokers. The best defence against excessive smoke, as any chain smoker will tell you, is to light up and provide your own smoke screen. All these customers obviously subscribed to this view.

Rex joined a table where a group of older men were gathered together. They were to become very familiar to Madge in the coming months. The table was filthy; drink-stained, littered with empty glasses, overflowing ashtrays, empty cigarette packets and wrappings. All the boys greeted Rex with loud jests, jovial insults of a marital nature and happy home of the double entendre. Rex really came alive; his enjoyment was evident as he parried the thrusts of innuendo about his rusty sexual prowess.

No show without punch, Madge thought, wincing at the crudities. After half an hour, her eyes began to sting and water, but Madge was beginning to learn a painful lesson; for Rex, the evening was merely beginning.

After the initial greeting from the boys, she was totally ignored, the complete fish out of water.

After a while, another man joined the group, if anything he was even older than Rex and the boys, but he bothered to take notice of Rex's young wife. He didn't try to make any smart remarks. He just asked Madge about her job and her family and pointed out that soon things would settle down. Marriage was a tremendous change for anyone.

Grateful to find a sympathetic ear, Madge chatted animatedly to this man just as she would to her father. Time flew. Unfortunately, Madge failed to notice Rex's expression becoming more and more thunderous as the evening progressed although he kept up an incessant flow of conversation of which he was the centre. He kept glancing over to check on Madge's conversation and evident absorption in her companion.

When the time came to leave, they all rose, vacating the pub and taking their leave outside with loud laughter and final insults. Rex began to walk swiftly away in the direction of the bedsit. Madge had to actually break into a run to keep up with him. He didn't answer her pleas to slow down or when she asked what crime she had committed. On arrival in the flat, Rex rounded on his young wife with a face white with anger and told her that she was never to humiliate him again in such a fashion.

Madge protested that she was only being polite and that his friend was only being kind by talking to her. For her pains, she received a short sharp slap on the cheek. Madge staggered back and burst into tears, whereupon Rex brushed past her and went to bed. When Madge joined him, after sitting quietly recovering, wrestling with this new side of her husband, he was already asleep.

The next day, Rex was quiet, terribly apologetic. In fact, he was as attentive a bridegroom as any bride could wish. His love-making that evening was tender, considerate and restrained. Madge became convinced that her wedding night and the next evening were a mere lapse in an otherwise satisfactory relationship.

'Let's take a couple of days off and go down to Bexhill-on-Sea. I have a couple of friends down there. The change will do you good,' Rex said by way of an apology.

Madge's heart lifted. This was more like the old Rex; perhaps the other night was indeed an isolated incident. They arrived in Bexhill around noon.

'My friends will be in the local,' Rex said, heading for the nearest pub.

These friends of Rex's were even older than him, Madge judged, especially as a lot of the talk was of World War I and the part they all played in it. Madge felt unable to contribute anything to the conversation, so she sat sipping her orange juice and gazing into space.

When they arrived back in London, Rex ordered his young wife, 'Put your luggage in the left luggage. I need a drink.'

Obediently, Madge did as she was told. A couple of hours later, when Rex could be persuaded to leave the pub, they returned to the left luggage office. Frantically, Madge searched through her bag for her ticket with no success, 'I've lost my ticket, Rex.'

'You surprise me,' Rex said ironically.

Madge appealed to the attendant, 'I'm so sorry I've lost my ticket.'

The woman indicated the rows and rows of luggage stacked up to the ceiling, 'What do you expect me to do about it love? There's a war on, in case you didn't know.'

'I'm sorry, but I wonder if you could look out for it? It has my name on the label.'

'Okay, love, give us the info.'

Early Days

When the couple came back from Bexhill, Madge had to face the harsh fact that Rex was an alcoholic and had been for a long time. It was a rude awakening, as he had kept the fact carefully hidden during their abbreviated courtship.

There was never enough money for food. Madge was never allowed to spend any money and Rex demanded her wages as soon as she was paid. He told her that she was too young to handle the money and because her suitcase had been mislaid, she only had the clothes she stood up in.

Rex had told her that he had a private income from his grandmother, but Madge never saw any evidence of it. Only the fact that Madge was young and strong helped her through the days that followed. There was only one bright spot in her life, Rex's family had always kept and bred whippets. So the day Rex walked through the door with a young whippet in tow, Madge was delighted. The young dog's bright intelligent eyes and loving nature were a source of great comfort to young Madge.

Before her honeymoon leave was over and with a heavy heart, Madge went out to the local post office and sent a telegram home. Terse and to the point it said:

Married in haste, repent at leisure. Love Madge.

During those first few weeks of marriage, Madge did not feel very well. It was nothing that she couldn't cope with but the work on the ward was very demanding. She just felt very tired. When she confided in Rosie, Rosie's eyes widened, 'You don't think you could be expecting a baby, Madge?'

'No, I haven't been married long enough, have I?'

'It's been known,' Rosie said knowingly.

'What will I do?'

'Wait and see,' said Rosie.

Wearily Madge let herself into the depressing little bedsit. The shift in the hospital had seemed endless. Now she had to do a quick change and keep a doctor's appointment. She was almost certain that she was expecting a baby and she was proved right. But the prospect wasn't as joyous as she had imagined it would be. Now she had to tell Rex, but she was still upset about the terrible row they had had the day before when she had decided to tackle him about all the things that had distressed her.

Since the day that they had married, Rex had given up all pretence of sobriety. He remained fairly sober at work, but evenings and weekends were spent in the local pub. Sometimes, he was spending as much as £5 a night, before reeling home to his resentful young wife.

Nearly at the end of her tether, Madge pleaded, 'Please, please, stop drinking, Rex. I don't understand why you do it.'

Rex wheeled round his red eyes glittering, 'Why? Why? You're just a child. You wouldn't understand even if I told you!'

'What I don't understand is why you married me. It hasn't made you happy and it's made me very unhappy. What did you hope to achieve?' Madge asked in desperation.

Rex shrugged his shoulders, 'Hoping for a miracle I suppose. I'm sorry I fell so short of your expectations.'

The row escalated with Madge complaining about the late-night card games with his undesirable friends, the fact that she had no clothes or shoes to wear, the shortage of food and having no money. All these things came tumbling out leaving her angry and trembling, close to tears. Rex listened in silence. When Madge's anger petered out, defeated by his stony silence, Rex looked at her and said, 'Are you finished?'

When Madge nodded dejectedly, he quietly left the flat.

Later that night, he returned. He lurched into the bedroom and stood surveying his sleeping wife, his bloodshot eyes vindictive. Roughly shaking her awake, Rex launched into a loud defence of his lifestyle, his friends, his freedom, adding that she was no help to him. To emphasise his points, Rex thumped his fist repeatedly on the bedside table. 'Thump, thump, thump!'

Later the following day, when Rex returned from work, he was surprisingly gentle when Madge told him that she was expecting his child.

'I will have to write to my mother. She'll be delighted. She doesn't even know that I got married,' Rex remarked.

True to his word, he sat down after dinner to write his letter. He was interrupted by a loud knock on the door. On answering, he turned to tell Madge that he was ordered to return to the waterworks, pronto.

After he had gone, Madge sat looking at the letter sitting on the table. Eventually, her curiosity overcame her, she picked the letter up and scanned the contents. He had addressed his mother as Darling Mummy; a few lines caught her attention, *She is not the cream of society and she's had no previous affairs.*

For a long time, Madge sat lost in thought. For the first time, she realised that she actually knew nothing at all about the kind of man she had married, and now there was a child on the way. Her eyes welled up, and slowly, a tear slid down her cheek.

Madge's first real assignment was to work in the male chronic tubercular ward in virtually isolated conditions from the rest of the hospital, where most of the patients were elderly. The exceptions being a couple of young soldiers sent home from the front. The work was hard, the standards exacting, the matron forbidding, but in many ways, the rigid discipline came as a relief from the uncertainties of life at home. She struck up an unexpected friendship with one of the young soldiers. He was by far the weaker of the two lads, but his face always brightened when Madge appeared on the ward, whichever shift she was working on.

Many whispered conversations took place between Wally and Madge while she held his pitifully thin wrist in her strong young fingers. Two troubled youngsters finding comfort in each other in a topsy-turvy world.

She learned that Wally was born and brought up in one of Manchester's tiny back-to-back terraces. His mother worked hard to bring up and feed eight kids while his father remained unemployed, pleading a bad back with consummate skill. Wally was the eldest child and the focus of his father's frustration, boredom and disappointment in life. Relations between father and son deteriorated to such an extent that

Wally joined the army as soon as he possibly could, even resorting to lying about his age by quite a few months.

Once in the army life improved immeasurably for the boy, the same army life that was so tough for some was idyllic by comparison with the conditions at home. Unfortunately, it was to be all too short-lived because Wally developed a racking cough aggravated by years of poor nutrition. At night, he was pelted with any handy missiles his exhausted mates could find as the poor lad tried to stifle his cough, until one night his staff sergeant, passing an open window, made a few discreet enquiries, whereupon Wally very swiftly found himself in the army field hospital and from there, he was transferred to St Thomas's.

Madge also learned in the course of their conversations that although not afraid of death itself, Wally had a morbid fear of dying alone. He was well aware that his condition was terminal, yet still he made pathetic attempts to hide bright spots of red blood that appeared on his handkerchiefs. Madge's heart went out to the lad when he told her that he had written to his mother, but so far there had been no reply, a circumstance he dismissed lightly by saying that his mother was no great shakes at writing. No doubt she had more important things to do.

One evening, when reporting for the night shift, Madge learned that Wally had taken a turn for the worse. Indeed, his flushed face and rapid pulse told their own story.

'Promise me something, Madge,' he asked in a hoarse whisper. 'If I die tonight, you will be there to hold my hand; I've just got to have somebody with me. Please, Madge. Please!'

Madge gently soothed his brow and reassured him that of course, he wasn't going to die, but she would be near him all night. Fortunately, her fellow worker that night was Rosie, who was understanding when Madge approached her and explained the circumstances.

'I'll keep cavey for you so that you can stay with him. Are you sure that's all that's in it?' Rosie asked slyly.

'Oh, you are a pal,' Madge pressed Rosie's hand gratefully, aware that if they were caught there would be serious consequences.

The night passed slowly. Wally tossed and turned fitfully, his breathing shallow. Madge left his side only to join Rosie and do regular checks on the rest of the ward. Several times, she caught Wally lying with his eyes wide open, relaxing only when he realised that she was nearby. Dawn arrived in a pink glow glimpsed from the high hospital windows and Madge relaxed for the first time that night. In her experience, albeit limited, patients rarely died once they had passed the crucial middle of the night, at least until the later in the day.

So, at 7 o'clock, when the shift changed and reports on the night's events were recorded, Madge slipped away to freshen up and change into "civvies". A light tap on the door of the nurse's station and an urgent whisper from Rosie reached her as she wearily climbed out of her uniform. Hastily pulling up one stocking, she sped semi-barefoot back to the ward where she stood helplessly gazing at Wally's still, pale face.

'I'm sorry, I didn't realise,' Rosie whispered. 'He died so quietly that he was gone before I noticed.'

'What on earth are you doing on the ward half-dressed, Macdonald?' the staff nurse snapped.

Too upset to reply, Madge gathered up her belongings and quickly walked away, leaving poor Rosie to explain. It seemed to Madge that life had hit an all-time low. Nothing seemed to be going right. She had failed Wally and it would seem she had failed Rex too. Tears stung her eyes as she walked slowly home. Normally, a girl who walked with her head held high and a spring in her step; today, her bowed head and stooped shoulders declared more than anything else her state of mind.

On arrival home, Madge exchanged a few brief words of greeting with Rex, before calling the whippet Toby to heel and going out for a long walk to give her time to think and rationalise her position. As she strolled along, eyes bent on the pavement, a hand caught her arm and she spun round in alarm.

'Madge, is it really you?' a familiar voice hailed her.

'Reg! Oh, Reg,' her depression lifted as if by magic. She threw her arms around her beloved brother and hugged him close.

'Steady on, old girl,' Reg said laughing.

'Oh, I'm just so glad to see you, Reg.'

'I traced you through the nurses' home,' Reg said after the initial hugs and kisses. 'Why on earth didn't you tell us that you were getting married? You must have missed out on a load of wedding presents. Some of the family might even have managed to come and wish you luck!'

Chattering nineteen to the dozen, they walked back to the bedsit to meet Rex, but Rex had slipped out for a moment. Still teasing his sister about keeping the family in the dark, Reg made himself comfortable on the old couch. When he turned around, he was concerned to see that tears were filling

Madge's eyes and spilling silently down her cheeks, where she hastily rubbed them away.

'I'm sorry, Reg,' she explained, 'I lost a patient this morning. It's just the reaction.'

Reg was silent. Just then Rex returned. Reg was totally amazed. Surely, this old man couldn't be Madge's husband? But that would appear to be the case. The two men shook hands as they were introduced and then they proceeded to engage in a kind of verbal fencing, trying to score points off one another while discovering as much as they could in a short space of time.

After a while, Reg turned his attention to his sister telling her all the latest family news. Madge flicked a glance at Rex who was leaning forward listening intently, a frown creasing his brow, obviously wondering what she was going to say to her brother. Putting on a brave face, Madge brought her brother up to date on her married life or at least gave him a carefully edited version. When she had finished, Rex rose and took his leave explaining that his shift at the waterworks began in half an hour's time. With one last warning glower to his wife, he departed.

After he had gone, Reg proved that he knew his sister better than she gave him credit for. Under his gentle questioning, she poured out a story that both horrified and angered her young brother. Just the sheer relief of sharing her problems acted as a burden rolling off her shoulders although for some reason she did not feel that she could tell Reg about her pregnancy.

For the first time in months, Madge laughed spontaneously in answer to many of Reg's wisecracks. In fact, she looked so much better during their evening together that

Reg felt angrier than ever toward Rex. It was a very serious young man who sat down later that evening to write to his parents.

Dear Mum and Dad

Dear Mum and Dad,

I'm writing this letter to let you know how things are up here in London. The first thing that you will like to know is that I came to London for an interview and a medical examination, and I managed to pass both of them, so I expect my commission will come through at any moment. When I get it, I expect that I'll go on leave for a little while and I'll try to come up and see you again then.

Let me explain about Madge in London. I first of all took a taxi to the nurses' home and enquired for her there. I was informed that she had married and that Mr Macdonald had moved to Thames Ditton to guard the waterworks there and that Madge had gone with him. Well, I duly caught the train and travelled to Thames Ditton to find the waterworks. When I found them, I enquired for Mr Macdonald and was told his address.

On my way there I saw a girl in front of me with a whippet dog. On passing her, I recognised Madge. After the usual "hellos", she asked me to come to her place for a cup of tea. Well, I went and discovered that instead of a flat, I was shown into a bedsitting room. That was the first blow!

Well, I started in my usual breezy fashion to pull Madge's leg about her hasty marriage and the fact that she missed getting any wedding presents due to her cutting the family off, and I asked her what the idea was. To my great surprise, she burst into tears.

Well, I didn't know what to do. I just couldn't understand it and put it down to the fact that she had hastily married some young fellow and was having some little tiff, so I duly said something about it being all right and that she would get over it. Nothing more was said at that moment.

Then Mr Macdonald came in. I don't know who was more astonished, but I think he was—Madge says that for the first time since she met him, she saw him at a loss for words. He literally gaped. I found out later that he considers Madge an "orphan of the storm" and that she has nobody in this world to worry about her.

Well, now to describe Mr Macdonald—the first impression one gets of him is of course his age. He is at least 40. Madge says 39 but by the medals up I assumed that he was older than that. He has bad teeth and looks anything like an ideal match for Madge. He looks as if he has had a good time all his life. His hair is half grey and half brown, and he looks dirty—you know, grimy—as if a damn good wash would do him good.

He started off by talking down to me—the high horse stuff. I managed to climb onto an even higher horse and reduced him to silence. I'm afraid I became a little snobbish and lost him completely as a possible friend. In fact, I showed him that I cordially detested him in about the first five words that I spoke to him. After those words, I ignored him and talked to Madge.

After a time, Madge had to go out and get the kettle on, and he promptly excused himself to wash his hands. I heard later that he rushed to the kitchen and told Madge that she must not show me that she was unhappy and not to let him down at all.

By this time, the fat was completely in the fire and he retired for the rest of the evening back to his job at the waterworks. I didn't wait to see him in the evening. In fact, he stayed at the work all night. I think the shock was too much for him.

Now to describe how Madge lives, firstly, she has no money at all. He says she is too young to have any money. If she wants to have cakes for tea, he gives her the money and expects the change. When he takes her out which is very seldom, his only pleasure is to go along to some lounge of a pub and see the boys. His wife is expected to go along with him and drink with all the people there—a very expensive pleasure for him.

I hear that he has been known to spend as much as £5 in one night just treating the lads to whiskeys, brandies and cocktails. The snag is that he is very jealous and if Madge, who hates drinking, speaks to any of the men present, he takes her outside and lectures her in a nice sarcastic manner. All his friends are about the 40 mark so Madge gets little young company. He really is a pig.

This is how they probably got married. Madge met him while she was at the hospital just as she finished her preliminary examinations for a nurse. He spun her a wonderful tale about him and his people.

As far as I can gather, he is one of the "Macdonalds of the Isles". His people are fairly wealthy, in fact I believe they have pots of money. They're careful not to give any to him as they must know that he is unable to keep it. Well, he spun this yarn and left out all the worst parts. He stayed off beer and liquor and made Madge promise not to tell anyone at home about the coming marriage. He is a crafty pig because he knew if she told the family anything we would have investigated the whole thing and the marriage would have been off.

Madge found a letter he was writing to his mother, he described Madge as a "strong healthy girl" who had no previous affairs but who is not the "cream of society". I could ring the old so and so's neck. Incidentally, he has been married before and has one girl who is at boarding school at present. He has not introduced her to any of his people—he probably thinks she isn't good enough.

Now about Madge's clothes. She is still wearing exactly the same clothes as she wore when she was married. Her shoes; one pair has worn completely through and he bought her a cheap pair. That is the only thing he has bought her. When I was there, I gave her £2 for a wedding present to buy something for her in the way of some clothes. She hasn't even got a pair of gloves and she feels the cold, as you know.

He gets rations from the army and he gets money for living out. So, up to the present, he has spent exactly nothing on Madge at all. Quite a good bargain, isn't it? Then he complains that she is unhappy all the time and he can't understand it, even though Madge has told him that at least she wants to be covered decently.

At one time, she mislaid her luggage in London and had to go around for two months with only the clothes she stood up in. I could go on for hours writing about it, but I think I have said sufficient to show you Mr Macdonald in the true light—he wants poisoning, the slug.

He has only laid his hands on her once—he's crafty there too—that time was the second day they were married and that was because she was polite to one of his friends. He says she is bad-tempered and calls her all the worst names that he can lay his tongue to and he has quite a good assortment of names that he has picked up in his long life.

This was my advice to Madge. Run him bills, she has him nagging at her all the time about nothing, and if she runs him bills for clothes and an occasional hair wave and generally herself a bit smarter, then he would have something to nag about. The other thing I advised her to do was to write home and explain the whole thing.

I hope she has written and please for heaven's sake don't write and chew her up for past mistakes—you'll break the girl's heart if you do. She is honestly in very bad shape. She is obviously unhappy and really needs a mother and father's sympathy. It will help a lot.

She looked tons brighter after my visit: You can see he doesn't believe anything she says. He doesn't or didn't believe I was in the RAF. He doesn't think, although he didn't say so, that I'm going to get a commission—but I'll shake him when I'm next in town if there is no change. He doesn't think that we had any dogs. In fact, he is under the impression that Madge invented her family. Don, me and both of you are really figments of Madge's imagination. Great, isn't it?

The third piece of advice is that if he gets too unbearable and it's quite likely, I'll send Madge the fare home, and I'll send money home to keep her until she gets a job up there. I'm sorry that I promised her that without previously consulting you, but I know that you wouldn't turn her away whatever happens. Well, I'll leave it to you, but I expect to be free again soon, and I'll go and see her again. Please write to her if only to show her husband that she has a home to go to.

I'm sending a piece of silk home to you. I expect it will come in useful for something, and if you could squeeze something out of it for Madge, I should be very grateful—it's off an Aussie plane, a Sunderland that crashed. It's one-third of a parachute so that will give you some idea of the actual size of it. It's the finest silk even though it looks a bit rough at present, and if you run an iron over it or dye it another colour, you will find it will make up into quite nice things. I'm sending the chords of the parachute also. They will each stand a man's weight so they may be useful for something.

Well, I'll close now. I think I've broken the record for letters home, but I really had to give a report on the London situation. By the way, talking about the London situation, I spent two nights at the Regent Palace Hotel. I went to bed at 10:00 at night, and the raid started. There were crashes and bangs all night. I went to bed with the bombs all around me, and after a time, I decided to go to sleep, as if I was going to be killed I might as well die in bed.

When I went out in the morning, Piccadilly was roped off as a delayed action bomb had landed there. All the shop windows in Regent Street are smashed, and London is definitely the place for a holiday now. The next night, the raid was the same.

All is well, cheerio for the time being.

Reg

1940

WHOOOEEE! WHOOOEEE! The sound of the air raid siren beat down on the ears of the populace, a sound that began slowly until it built into an almost unbearable howl that was impossible to ignore. The London street was fairly quiet in the late evening; the sunlight had receded with the end of the rush hour and just a few stragglers hurried homeward.

Suddenly, the street came alive and doors opened all along the row. Londoners, by now well versed in the art of making the underground shelters comfortable, tumbled out onto the pavements carrying blankets, Lilos, eiderdowns, kettles, primus stoves and pillows, with one enterprising soul dragging a large mattress. Then they all disappeared down the subway like rabbits into their burrows at the first sign of danger.

In sharp contrast to the busy street scene, silhouetted against the window of her top-floor flat, a young woman stood very still and watched the tide of humanity rush to its intended destination. She felt alone, detached and isolated. The frantic activity and appalling noise had nothing to do with her.

'Mrs Macdonald! Mrs Macdonald!' The harsh tones of her landlady broke through Madge's reverie, 'It's time to go!'

Hurrying to the top of the stairs, Madge called down, 'Okay, Mrs Jenkins. I'll follow you down in a minute.'

Madge winced and put her hands over her ears in a vain attempt to block out the insistent sound of the siren. Returning to the window, she heard the front door slam and watched the tiny figure of her landlady join the throng.

What on earth am I doing? Madge mused; *I'm terrified of the bombs. Now I'll probably be killed.*

Instinctively, she touched her stomach gently as if to reassure the unborn child. Although very fearful of the bombs, she couldn't bear the thought of having to face the obstinately cheerful figures of her neighbours and acquaintances, showing the kind of courage and resilience for which Londoners became famous. It was more than that though. She was three months' pregnant, and the feeling of nausea was very strong within her, so the thought of the crowded underground station made her gorge rise. So many people, the air of bewilderment, the crying children, the sharp-tongued mothers, the distinct odour of massed humanity united by fear.

Ashamed of those unworthy thoughts, Madge realised that she had another very good reason for not joining her fellows in the shelter. Mrs Jenkins was very curious about Madge and invariably spent the long hours of enforced intimacy attempting to engage her quiet tenant in conversation and so to reveal any secrets she was sure the girl harboured.

Madge often found herself open to attack as her landlady prodded and pried into her private life, the temptation to tell the old lady to mind her own business was overwhelming, but to give in to it would be to jeopardise her position as a tenant.

Fencing questions as politely as she could and acutely aware of many listening ears only too glad to have something to relieve the boredom, Madge was always profoundly grateful to hear the "ALL-CLEAR", which meant that she could escape to her room.

Suddenly, she realised that the street was completely deserted, from chaos came calm. The staccato note of the siren died slowly away and all was quiet. Then, gradually on the very limit of human perception, a new sound became audible, a low droning hum, freezing the very marrow of the listener. Madge felt the stirrings of real fear.

Being a fatalist was one thing, but tempting fate was another. The German Air Force had arrived. The sound was not a new one; London had been subjected to almost continual bombing raids for the past few months, but this time it was different. They came to deliver an even more hellish cargo; the firebombs were making their debut and the blitz had begun.

The terrifying sound of falling bombs made Madge shrink away from the window. Slowly, a weird light spread from the east, bathing London in a warm glow. The gentle light shone into the dingy room, softening the hideous wallpaper and masking the threadbare carpet, throwing the damp discoloured ceiling into shadow and touching the side of the faded bedspread. Madge almost warmed to the place until a bright blinding flash of light sharply illuminated the stark reality of the bedsit.

Hastily, she drew the blackout blind down and shut out the fearful scene. Putting on the electric light, she sat on the bed and slowly sank onto the pillows gazing around at the now familiar room with its tiny adjoining kitchen. The dark brown varnished wallpaper embellished with raised patterns and faded floral designs must have been purchased at least half a century ago and the frequent wetting of the paper around the sink area had caused it to lift and bubble.

In several places, long strips of wallpaper had been torn off, adding to the general air of neglect. The dark brown doors, the cracked glass of the light shade, graveyard of a thousand flies. The old tin bucket in the corner for use as an emergency toilet should the communal bathroom be occupied, as was invariably the case. The stained carpet, threadbare tracks showing the movement of countless tenants.

Madge felt a slow tear falling down her cheek, which she firmly brushed away. *I won't give way to something that is no more than self-pity*, she thought. It's only because I'm pregnant and can't face cleaning up the place that it looks so dismal.

Suddenly, a particularly loud explosion startled her. The house shook and she grasped the top pillow and folded it tightly over her ears like a gigantic bonnet. For the first time, the enormity of her position and the vulnerability of her unborn child forcibly struck her. Trying not to panic, she hastily gathered her bedding and squeezed under the solid iron bedstead, preparing to wait out the raid.

For the first few minutes, every sound made her jump nervously, her imagination working overtime. But she gradually relaxed and half-awake, half-asleep, the sounds of war receding, her mind began to drift back to happier times.

Scotland

The Forth Bridge towered above them: The wind was warm, and the fluffy summer clouds scudded across the uncharacteristically deep blue sky. *When Scotland has good weather, it must be the best place in the world to be*, Madge thought. She sighed contentedly as she lay outstretched with her hands behind her head, utterly relaxed, her eyes closed.

Beside her, George on his front studied her face intently, 'Did you know that you have the most incredibly long eyelashes?'

'Careful or I'll sweep you away,' said Madge laughing.

She felt comfortable with George. She felt she had known him all her life, and in point of fact, she almost had although he was a friend of Don's and had been since primary school days. Lilian and Harry had always included George in most of the family activities, one of which was about to take place that very day. But this was private time for the two young people. Madge was aware that George was troubled about his school career.

Don had passed all his "Highers" and as a consequence had gone to study medicine at Edinburgh University. George too had passed all his "Highers" with distinction with the exception of his "bête noire", Latin. His headmaster had pleaded with the education board to give the boy another chance because he felt that he was brilliant although it meant that George would have to take every subject over again. George felt that this was a huge responsibility; his headmaster's faith in him was awesome to the young man.

'I know I can pass all the subjects again, Madge. I know I can, but I'm not that sure about the Latin, as you know I really need Latin to study medicine, and I'm terrified in case I let the Head down.'

'You won't let him down, George,' Madge said emphatically. 'You are well worth a second chance.'

'If I don't pull it off this time, I'll probably have to go into banking,' George said gloomily. 'What a dreadful prospect!'

'Oh, I don't know,' Madge, said playfully. 'You could always give me a loan, interest-free.'

'My interest in you is always free,' George became serious for a moment. 'I really like you and I live in hope that you will learn to like me a bit too.'

'I do like you George. You're the best friend I could wish to have,' Madge replied, then sensing that the moment was becoming too serious she sat up straight. Coming to her feet in one graceful movement, she extended her hand to George to pull him to his feet, 'We have to join the others now. Mum has planned a bramble ramble after our swim.'

'Well, I guess have to get a move on then. She who must be obeyed has spoken,' George said with a smile. He had known Lilian of old for many years.

The hut the family rented for the summer was tucked in the trees, reached by a little path ending in a wooden gate. In front of the hut was a kind of two-tier grassy bank; in the corner, Harry was patiently trying to light a small fire. Don was sprawled on his stomach, deep in a book. Reg laid beside his father blowing enthusiastically to try and coax some kind of life from the flickering flames. Brenda was sitting on the bank sorting out a bunch of wildflowers she had been gathering.

Just as Madge and George arrived, Lilian came out of the hut with a beach towel slung over her shoulders, 'For goodness sake, Harry, leave the wretched fire alone; otherwise, we'll be here all day,' she complained. 'We can light the primus.'

'Well,' said Don, 'this won't get the sea peopled with eager bathers, will it? Last in gets to do the washing up!'

With this dire threat issued the five young people flew out of the gate, down the path, over the sand and into the icy water. Gasping and spluttering there then ensued a friendly argument as to who was the laggard. Reg was last; they all agreed.

'That's not fair!' Reg moaned. 'I stood on a sharp stone.' He showed his injured foot to meet with scant sympathy.

'Never mind Reg,' said Madge laughing. 'You don't have to wash up with your feet.'

Still laughing over Reg's misfortune the young people were joined in the water by Lilian and Harry. Lilian was still undeniably a fine figure of a woman although she was the mother of four young adults; her ruched swimsuit clung to every firm curve.

'Come on, everyone!' Lilian said firmly, pulling on her close-fitting rubber-swimming cap. Fastening the snap under her chin, she waded into the freezing waters of the Firth of Forth. It was one of her unwavering family rules that a trip to the beach included a compulsory swim for everyone, even her cairn terrier. Doing a sedate breaststroke, she swam out for 300 yards, comically accompanied by the bobbing head of the small cream-coloured dog.

Harry passed her several times going back and forth doing an enthusiastic if unskilled crawl. The youngsters were all fairly accomplished swimmers; they swam steadily out to sea until a warning shout from Don made them turn back towards the distant shoreline.

'Time for tea!' Lilian called when everyone had emerged from the water and made their way back up the path.

Wrapped in towels they all sat sipping the hot tea and eating their prepared rolls.

'Tastes good,' George murmured.

'Sorry about the Highers, old man,' Don consoled his old friend. 'You'll get them next time for sure. I'll keep a place at university warm for you.'

'Yes,' chimed in Madge, 'that's what I've been trying to tell him!'

'You'll only be a year ahead of me,' Reg said. 'That's real hard luck to have to redo a year at school.'

'I think it's a great idea! I expect Madge will think the same, which means you'll be around for the next year, George,' Brenda said slyly.

'Little girls should be seen and not heard, young Brenda,' said Reg, dodging swiftly as Brenda threw the dregs of her teacup in his direction.

'Now now, children,' Lilian cut in, 'get dressed, and when Reg has finished the washing up, we'll each take a basket and go for a bramble ramble.'

A chorus of groans greeted this suggestion, but obediently, the family dressed and assembled together outside the hut.

'Mum looks a picture of sartorial elegance, doesn't she?' whispered Reg, giggling.

It is worth noting that Lilian had been born into a generation that had never known what it was like to wear trousers. In fact, she didn't even own a pair so in order to protect her legs from the vicious bramble bushes and nettles, and she carefully wrapped each leg in newspapers tied on with string. Glaring around at the suppressed giggles reflected in each merry face, Lilian stomped off followed by her family; she looked for the world like a mother duck and her ducklings going to water.

Over the years, the "bramble ramble" had grown into quite a competitive race. Each family member determined to outdo the others. This race was quietly fuelled and fostered by Lilian, who generally managed to make enough jam to see the family through the winter and instil a lifelong aversion to blackberry jam in everyone who participated. Occasional shouts rang out over the hillside as the young people kept in touch. One of the unwritten rules of the bramble rambles was that one never returned to base until one's basket was brimming.

On this occasion, Madge was lucky she found a particularly productive fruit bush simply groaning with the ripe blackberries. So, swiftly filling her basket, she returned to base early, just in time to be treated to the spectacle of her mother rapidly disappearing down the hill on her behind, to end with each newspapered leg wrapped round a large tree trunk. All her berries strewn behind her like a rich red carpet.

Hurrying forward, stifling her hysterical laughter, Madge moved to help Lilian to her feet.

'Leave me alone!' Lilian snapped, furious and humiliated that Madge had witnessed her undignified fall.

Wisely Madge left her mother to struggle up unaided. It was very late by the time the family eventually arrived home, but Lilian would not let anyone go to bed until every bramble had been washed and prepared for the great jam-making session the following day.

Lying in their shared bedroom much later, Brenda asked, 'Do you like George, Madge?'

'Course, I do,' said Madge.

'But do you love him?'

'Goodnight, Brenda.'

"Bang, bang, bang!" Madge woke with a start and realised that someone was banging on the door. Calling out that she was coming, Madge eased herself out from under the bed and opened the front door. Reg almost fell into the room.

'What on earth are you doing Madge? Mrs Jenkins tells me that you didn't go down to the shelters when the raid started.'

His eyes fell on the pillow and bedding, 'Good heavens! You've been under the bed?'

'I just couldn't face the crowds in the shelter. I'm pregnant, Reg.'

'Pregnant, how long?'

'Three months.'

'Well, that settles it,' Reg said firmly. 'You can't stay here like this. You have the child to consider now. I was going up to Scotland anyway, and you are coming with me.'

Madge found her voice, 'But what about Rex?'

'Damn Rex!' Reg almost shouted. 'You owe him nothing Madge; he should have made sure you and the child were safe. These are firebombs those Huns are dropping; London is on fire. We've got to go now; trains are leaving for the North all the time. I've got a week's leave, Mum and Dad are expecting me, so get your case packed.'

Galvanised by the urgency in his voice, Madge opened her suitcase and threw her pitifully few belongings into it. Finally, she wrote a note to Rex explaining the situation and placed it propped up on the table. Then, together, Madge and Rex hurried down the stairs past Mrs Jenkins' inquisitive gaze and out into the crowded London.

The Train Journey

Reg and Madge stood for a moment inside the vast arch of London's Kings Cross station, looking at the heaving crowd of humanity rushing hither and thither. Servicemen, servicewomen, civilians, crocodiles of bewildered children with prominent identifying labels pinned to their lapels, porters laden with bags. It seemed to Madge that the entire population of London was gathered under one roof. The noise was deafening too, piercing whistles, shunting trains, steam emissions, shouted instructions, crying children. It felt like a solid wall of sound beating down on their senses.

Reg took a firm hold of Madge's hand and together they plunged into the maelstrom, threading their way through to the enormous timetable and standing with other anxious travellers scanning the board for their eventual destination.

'There it is!' Reg said excitedly. 'Oh, my word, it leaves in four minutes!'

With that, both of them flew to their waiting train, hurrying down the endless platform, wrestling open the heavy carriage door and falling thankfully into the long narrow corridor. For a moment or two, they stood catching their breath before becoming aware of their surroundings. The entire corridor was packed with suitcases, each pile with an owner perched on top. Reg stood assessing the situation as the train suddenly lurched violently forward and the journey began.

It was unthinkable to Reg that Madge should spend the greater part of the long journey ahead sitting on her suitcase even if the thin battered relic could bear her weight. So he began to examine each carriage in detail. As expected, each one was completely occupied. In some, the armrests had been pushed back, and the seats held four uncomfortable-looking adults on each side. But, at last, there was a chink of light. In the last carriage, there was a possibility of providing a seat if everyone could be persuaded to move up. Reg pulled the heavy carriage doors apart and six pairs of eyes swung towards him.

'Excuse me, I wonder if you would consider moving up to let my sister sit down? She is not very well. We are going to Waverley and it's a long way to go without a seat.'

Without complaint, a space appeared and Reg settled Madge into it before returning to sit on his suitcase.

Madge really hadn't had time to consider the enormity of her actions since Reg burst into her bedsitter in the early hours of the morning, and now the full impact of what she had done hit home. Guilt about Rex, how this would affect the future of her child and apprehension about the kind of welcome which awaited her at home. Her eyes filled with prickling tears.

Fumbling in her bag, she realised with horror that she had left her handkerchief behind and her nose began to run freely. Three pairs of eyes stared impassively from the opposite seats; her misery was now complete. Succour came from an unexpected source. The very old gentleman sitting on Madge's right wordlessly proffered his snow white handkerchief. She took it gratefully offering a watery smile of thanks. Then resting her head against the rough fabric of the carriage seat, she closed her eyes and tried to relax.

Meanwhile, outside the compartment, Reg sat on his case dozing lightly. He jerked awake suddenly, conscious that he was not alone. A young man of about the same age stood pressed against the train window in a position of utter dejection. Reg gazed at him in astonishment. Remarkably, the young man's arms were extended in a crucifix position each arm bound in rigid splints attached to a kind of yoke affair, which passed around the back of his neck, 'Are you all right?' Reg asked, aware that it was an inane question but unsure how to proceed.

'Do I look it?' the young man said ruefully.

'Come to mention it; you don't really,' Reg said apologetically. 'Can you sit down?'

'I think so.'

So saying, the young man carefully lowered himself onto one of the innumerable suitcases blocking the corridor. His name was Andrew, Reg discovered, and he was on his way back home to Edinburgh.

To while away the long journey, Reg told Andrew about Madge and the hasty decision to return home. Andrew nodded sympathetically, and in return, he told Reg a fascinating tale of his wartime exploits and how he came to be in such a fix. His regiment had been posted to Norway, and he was sent to the front immediately to lead an assault team, a task that delighted the young man; he was eager to get to grips with the enemy. Had he been more experienced, however, perhaps he might have taken a more cautious approach to a potentially dangerous situation. As it was, he crested the brow of a hill only to be mown down by an unseen enemy.

He was very badly hurt indeed, his arms and upper body taking the full blast of the shell. Hastily companions dragged him out of danger, screaming for a stretcher bearer, but the most amazing thing Andrew told Reg was that at no time since being hit did he lose consciousness—during the rough journey over the snow-covered terrain to reach the first aid tent, he felt every jolt, the feeling of almost being tipped off his precarious perch, the numbness of his body. At last, the trip was over, and it was with a great sigh of relief that Andrew felt the surgeon running his hands over his body, assessing, deciding. Then to his absolute horror, the surgeon turned to his orderly and said, 'Take this one outside. He's too badly injured. There are others I can save, but if he's still alive in the morning, I will see what I can do.'

Andrew opened his mouth to make a loud protest but no sound was forthcoming; nothing worked, so it was with a sense of unreality and utter despair that he found himself being wheeled outside the operating room. It was the longest night that he could ever remember in his life.

As the pale fingers of dawn crept into the cracks around the tent, the orderly returned to make a cursory examination of the man lying motionless on the stretcher. Astonished, he called out to the operating room.

'This one's still alive, sir!'

'Wheel him in,' came the tired reply.

'I was eventually taken to the vet's hospital in Kent,' Andrew continued. 'After I began to recover a bit, I began to think about my wife back in Edinburgh. Somehow, I couldn't bear the thought of returning to her not as a whole man. So I sat down and wrote to her, saying that I would just disappear and that she was not to look for me because life would never be the same for us. My scars were horrendous; I only had two fingers on my right hand, and three on my left. What sort of job could I expect with that sort of injury?'

Reg shook his head slowly, 'Did she reply?'

'Almost immediately, she was very cross with me. She told me that "of course, I was to come home. There was no question of disappearing," so as you can see here I am,' Andrew said ruefully, shrugging his shoulders.

'But why did the hospital discharge you with this awful apparatus?' Reg asked curiously.

'I'm afraid it was a case of needs must, there were new cases arriving every day, so anyone they could crank to their feet was discharged.'

'Well, it must be difficult to get about. Speaking of getting about, would you like a cup of tea?' he asked.

'Not right now, old man. It only causes problems, if you know what I mean,' Andrew looked rueful.

'Oh, I see,' said Reg.

'Do you want to go now?'

'I don't think I will be able to get to the toilet,' Andrew replied.

'Well, nothing ventured,' Reg said leading the way, followed by an ungainly sideways shuffle. With Reg holding the door open, Andrew tried to position himself over the toilet bowl, but they discovered that even with the door open the toilet was too small to accommodate Andrew's splints.

'I guess you will just have to cross your legs, old man,' Reg grinned, 'at least until we get to York and that's two hours away.'

Eventually, the train reached York station and the two young men headed straight to the station toilets. They arrived at the urinals, Reg remaining behind to give Andrew some privacy. When he caught sight of a strange expression on Andrew's face, part pleading and part apology, he realised what he was required to do. Silently, cursing his stupidity, Reg moved forward to lend a helping hand.

Due to the large number of people leaving at York, the rest of the trip was spent in relative comfort in the same carriage with Madge, the three young people trying to block out their troubles with light-hearted banter and careless teasing until they parted at Waverley Station never to meet again.

Home

The taxi drew up outside the small terraced Council house in Rosyth. Madge grabbed Reg's arm, 'What do you think Mum will say?'

'Don't worry. She'll be fine. After all, it's not as if you could help any of this,' Reg reassured her.

Lilian answered the door; her expression tight-lipped. Without a word of welcome, she stepped aside and allowed her daughter and son to enter the house. As Reg passed her, he asked his mother in a low tone, 'Did you get my letter?'

'Yes,' said Lilian.

When they were all gathered in the lounge, Lilian turned to ask Madge, 'I just hope you know what you are doing, Madge. Your dad and I can't keep you, you know.'

Madge began to speak, but Reg forestalled her, 'This will help over the first few weeks,' so saying, Reg reached into his wallet and handed over a small roll of notes to his mother, 'It's not much, but it will help. I don't think Madge has got any of her own.'

'I don't doubt it,' Lilian sniffed.

Madge flashed Reg a grateful glance.

After a fortifying cup of tea, Madge brought her parents up to date on the whole sorry saga of her marriage. Several times, Lilian began to interrupt, but she subsided after a warning frown from Harry. It was only when Madge admitted that she was pregnant that the full significance of her daughter's plight was brought home to her.

'You're pregnant,' Lilian said sharply, 'when is it due?'

'About the middle of March,' Madge said quietly.

'So you're three months gone? Well, this is a fine kettle of fish,' Lilian said, ignoring Reg's warning glance. 'We know nothing about this man Rex. You've got no job, no prospects being as you are. If you don't go back to that husband of yours, then who's going to look after the child when you go back to work? That's what I'd like to know?'

'Now then Lily,' said Harry calmly, knowing how much she hated the diminutive, 'you're taking a very gloomy view. Perhaps this Rex fellow will come to take Madge home as soon as he realises she's gone. Perhaps this is just the kind of shock the fellow needs to be able to pull himself together and stop all this drinking lark. In any case, this is Madge's home and as such, she is always very welcome here whatever the circumstances.'

Lilian fell silent.

After a couple of days, during which Madge had time to sort herself out, catch up on some much-needed rest, recharge her batteries and spend some time wondering what on earth to put in a letter to Rex. Eventually, she took her courage in both hands and drawing a writing pad towards her, began to write.

'Dear Rex,

I'm so sorry I had to leave so suddenly before I could let you know, but Reg felt that London was just too dangerous for me to stay any longer. I know you would have agreed if you had been there. The air raid was really quite frightening. I am keeping quite well; the doctor tells me that the expected date of confinement is 14 March.

I hate to ask, but I wonder if you could see your way to sending me a little money so that I can have some independence from my parents? They are not, as you know, very well off, and it would enable me to buy a few baby clothes. Then hopefully, I can get a job after the baby has been born. I am hoping my mother will look after the baby during the day. I don't think she is very keen on the idea, but perhaps she will change her mind.

I suppose there is no news about when your regiment is due to go to India. Do you think that when the war is over, we can review the situation and reconsider our lives together, who knows, maybe we can start afresh, what do you think?

Reg has written to say that he visited you recently and you both had "words". I just hope he wasn't too nasty. He's only trying to protect me, and sometimes, he can get carried away.

How is life otherwise? We read about the blitz in the newspapers. London seems such a dangerous place at the moment.

Take care of yourself, till we meet again.

Your loving wife,
Marjorie.
Xxxxxxx'

Several days passed. Anxiously, she watched the mail wondering what Rex was doing, whether his draft had come through, thinking that her father had been right and the shock of her leaving had made Rex give up the drink. The silence from Rex was deafening.

Christmas was fast approaching and in her straitened circumstances, Madge managed to get a temporary job in one of the stores in town for the Christmas period only. It wasn't a sinecure, but it was better than nothing. It got her out of the house and away from Lilian for most of the day as well as relieving the financial pressure.

It was her day off. Madge had forgotten how cold it could be in December on the east coast of Scotland. She shivered as she clutched her thin coat closer to her body. A new coat was out of the question. It was five weeks since she and Reg had come back to surprise their parents. Reg had returned to London almost immediately and Madge missed him terribly. Faced with Lilian's thinly veiled hostility, she could badly use an ally. A spasm of coughing stopped her in her tracks. *That reminds me, I must get some cough medicine*, she thought.

Dunfermline reassuringly hadn't changed one iota since she last stood on this very spot what seemed like a lifetime ago. Ducking into a small café out of the bitter wind, Madge chose a small table near the window. Once settled, she took an envelope out of her pocket. It was from Rex and it had arrived that morning. She had sent four letters altogether trying to keep a note of real desperation out of the correspondence while still conveying a sense of urgency. Surely, Rex, with all his wealth of experience, would provide a workable solution? Her trembling fingers tore open the envelope.

The Letter...

My darling Marjorie,

I still cannot believe that you have done this to me. You can imagine my shock when I arrived home to find that you had deserted me. I find Mrs Jenkins' questions most embarrassing, and you have created a continuing nightmare for me, my darling.

But, despite everything, I still love you, fool that I am. I know you are anxious about the financial position, what with the coming child and everything. Well, my darling, would that I could shower you with presents and cheques to make your life more bearable, but unfortunately, several unforeseen bills have arrived taking what little I had saved up to send you. I cannot believe life is so cruel.

You will be very glad to hear that I got a very good write-up from my CO this time. They seem to have decided to overlook my peccadilloes in the past, so I'm hoping I'm top line for the captain's slot, possibly when I get to India. Be happy for me, my darling. Perhaps there is a future for us over the rainbow?

Thinking of you always,
Your very own, Rex.

Slowly, Madge crumpled the letter, kneading it between the palms of her hands until small pieces separated and fell onto her lap like confetti. Tears ran unchecked down her cheeks and despair enveloped her. Abruptly, she pushed her chair back and rushed blindly into the street.

'Madge!' a familiar voice hailed her. 'I don't believe it!'

Blinking her tears back, Madge realised that it was George bearing down on her. His hand outstretched, a beaming smile on his face. Madge froze, only too painfully aware of her swollen red eyes. Her fine hair plastered flat to her head. Her pregnancy announced by the fact that only the first two buttons on her coat were fastened.

'Oh, George,' she faltered, 'how nice to see you.'

'Let me introduce you to my wife, Melanie,' George pulled a very pretty blonde girl forward; she extended a limp hand for Madge to shake.

'We must get together for a chat,' George enthused.

'We have to go, darling. We have a train to catch,' George's wife reminded him.

'Yes, we'll have to chat.' Madge faltered. 'Perhaps we'll have a chance later on, I'm staying with my parents for a bit. I'm married too you know,'

Madge blushed scarlet. It seemed ridiculous to have to justify her condition like this.

'Yes, all right, Madge. You'll have to tell me all about this lucky fellow.'

Murmuring goodbyes, Madge scurried away, her burning face attracting a few mildly curious stares. Interested only in escape, Madge found her footsteps taking her towards Pittencrieff Glen, the beautiful wooded parkland donated by a former resident of Dunfermline, Andrew Carnegie.

Thankfully, she entered the hushed world she hadn't seen for a couple of years. Taking one of the quiet pathways at random, she wandered slowly around the peaceful glades.

Sheltered from the wind, she sat on a rustic bench watching the swiftly flowing brook, listening to the soothing sound of running water. Her thoughts wandered to the baby so soon to make an appearance. She felt a fierce wave of protective instinct flooding her body. *Whatever happens, I won't let you down*, she whispered.

Feeling a chill, she rose ungainly from the bench and made her way towards the familiar hot houses, where she spent quite some time wandering through the exotic vegetation, marvelling at the beautiful tropical blooms, enjoying the warm humid air.

Time seemed suspended; it was only when she emerged into the sharp December air that she realised that she was going to be late home. The day hadn't finished with her yet; Lilian was waiting for her to come through the door and she launched straight into the attack.

'Well, have you heard from that husband of yours?'

'Yes, Mum.'

'Well, go on. What did he say?'

'He said that he hasn't got any money at present.'

'And you believe that?'

'I don't know what to believe,' cried Madge in despair.

'I do,' said Lilian. 'You've been taken for a ride, my girl, and you've been left holding the baby. Well, don't expect us to support you after the baby's born. You'll have to get a proper job.'

The dawn rose like a gently lifted veil, slowly revealing harsh terrain, the barren rocks, the empty desert plains, the blond red sun rising swiftly to its zenith. Amid this uncompromising landscape the twentieth-century bustle of a full-blown Royal Artillery army camp.

Shouts echoed around the camp as groggy soldiers tried to jump to attention, struggling to put on the entirely unsuitable uniform for desert climes. Two officers stood just within the confines of one of the tents having a quiet smoke before breakfast. They were talking quietly about the plans for the day when Rex passed by half-dressed heading for his horses.

'What do you make of that Macdonald chappie?' asked the senior officer.

'I really don't know much about him, except that he's a bit of an oddball. He's an old man too, isn't he?'

'Well, he must be well over 40,' said the first officer, 'because I understand that he was in World War I. In fact, it is rumoured that he was so badly affected by the conditions during the war that he has never been quite the same since. I suppose that could explain his eccentric behaviour when he got into that bit of bother before we got posted out here. I was actually present when he made a complete ass of himself.'

'That was before I joined,' the younger man put in. 'What happened, or is it classified?'

'No, nothing like that.' Nevertheless, the officer's voice sank to a husky whisper, 'Apparently, old Rex got very drunk one evening, burst into the Officers' Mess and yelled, 'Once more into the breach dear friends! The Jerries are coming, or are they just breathing heavily?' Then he just leaned against the wall and giggled helplessly.

'All of which was inexcusable, of course, but it happened to be ladies' night and all the officers' wives were present. I have a feeling that old Macdonald was just about to be cashiered on the spot but for the intervention of the CO's wife. She simply led old Rex away and returned later to placate her irate old man. Turned out the lucky blighter only got a reprimand.'

'He was damned lucky the CO's wife spoke up for him then.'

'Oh, I don't think that had a lot to do with it,' the senior officer said shrewdly. 'He might be an oddball, who drinks like the dickens, but on the other hand, there's not a bloke in this regiment who can touch him when it comes to handling horses.'

Nodding in agreement the two men lapsed into companionable silence.

Rex's eyes softened as he slipped his arm around his favourite mare. She whickered softly, pushing her velvet nose under his chin as he stroked her ears gently in a loverlike gesture. Suddenly, without warning, the beautiful mare pushed enthusiastically, catching Rex unawares and almost unbalanced him. Laughing under his breath, the man moved on to greet his other charges.

Rex was especially excited this morning. He had just heard that he had been put in sole charge of the regimental mule pack. Dealing with animals was right up his street. It was a world he felt relaxed and confident in. Here, he could forget the cares of a harsh critical world. Later in the morning back in his tent, Rex picked up the letter lying on the truckle bed and read the contents again.

'Dear Rex,

I hope this letter reaches you as I haven't heard from you for such a long time. Rex, can we not put our differences to one side and consider the child Diane? As you can see from the enclosed photograph, she is a bonny baby. It's hard to believe that she is almost two years old. She is very good-tempered, and I can see a strong resemblance to you. Do you think so?

My mother has been nagging me to go and see our doctor for ages. There's obviously something wrong with me. I just feel that I want to drink and sleep all the time. It takes a real effort to eat anything at all so I'm beginning to look as if I could slip through the eye of a needle.

I don't know what he will suggest, but I'm getting to the point where I don't really care as long as I feel better than I do at present. However, enough of my troubles, I expect you've got more than enough of your own.

Love,
Madge.'

For a long moment, Rex stood staring at the letter in his hand, looking without seeing, thinking without understanding.

Then, heaving a deep sigh, he crossed the tent and groped under his bedding for the precious bottle, strange how a nip of whiskey helped clear the clouds away and concentrate the mind. He lay sprawled across the bed lost in contemplation and whiskey fumes.

India

Summoned to appear before his commanding officer, Rex stood to attention while his senior officer slowly leafed through the papers on his desk, deliberately keeping Rex waiting in the time-honoured fashion of senior to junior officers in the British army. At length, he looked up and said, 'We've received an order for 50 mules to be taken over the border to Burma. As you know, the Japs have captured Rangoon and Singapore, so our troops need our support. They have had to retreat across the Sittang River, which puts them within spitting distance of our position here.'

'Now what I want you to do, Captain, is take the overland route with the mules, crossing the border. After that, you are on your own I'm afraid. Your orders are to locate and supply the Essex Yeomanry with the mules. You'll have to keep a sharp lookout for Japs.'

'I understand the country is crawling with them and believe me they take no prisoners. They'd rather kill first, and by all accounts they're none too fussy about how they do it. I'm giving you Ranjit Singh; the border country is his home, so he can give you a fair idea of where to go. Any questions?'

'No, sir, thank you, sir,' Rex turned on his heel and marched out in search of Ranjit Singh.

The two men sat heads close together, one with grey-brown straight hair, the other a riot of blue-black curls. The map was spread between them as they tried to decide the best route to take over the mountain range, which bordered Assam, into the North West of Burma.

'The easiest route is by the Imphal plain, but it's also the best known and the Japs are bound to have it covered because of retreating soldiers as well as idiots like ourselves trying to get in.' Rex grinned at Ranjit. 'So what's the alternative old boy?'

With the characteristic solemnity of his race, Ranjit Singh pointed to the Naga mountain range, 'No one would expect us to come from this direction, boss.'

'Bloody hell!' Rex exploded. 'I shouldn't bally well think so either. We've got to take 50 mules remember!'

A grave pair of shining black eyes met Rex's own.

'It can be done,' said Ranjit Singh.

The next day was spent loading up all the animals with provisions, medicines, food and ammunition for the besieged troops. The mules were given a good feed and were well watered. They set off before dawn intent on getting the easiest part of the journey over under cover of darkness, leaving the long day for the rugged ascent. They had carefully planned their route, due mostly, it must be said to Ranjit's local knowledge, so that as dawn broke they found themselves in the foothills of the Naga Mountains.

Rex was beginning to feel the pace, he could give his companion at least fifteen years, but as he was the senior officer, any betrayal of weakness would result in a serious loss of face. Grasping the opportunity to stop on the pretext of admiring the view, Rex sat astride his mule, swivelling round in the saddle to get a better panoramic aspect, he caught his breath. All his time had been taken up with the sheer physical effort of negotiating the loose stones that littered the slopes, but by jingo, he was forced to admit that India was beautiful. Several streams were visible among the thick green forested areas. Many shades of green covered the valleys and hills of these attractive foothills.

Although they had left the hot dusty Indian plane behind, it still got pretty hot around midday. When Rex suggested to stop for a drink, Ranjit assented with a nod. So far, the mules had been exemplary; surefooted as they picked their way over the roughest of terrain. Finally, they stopped on the banks of a fast-running stream. After watering the animals, the two men sat companionably on the moss-covered banks. Rex smoked one of his cigarettes while Ranjit ate a pomegranate with great relish.

Not daring to linger too long they mounted their animals and set off again. Now the terrain was distinctly rougher. The green gradually gave way to scrubby plants. The steepness of the climb tested the strength and stamina of all the mules. Ranjit was in front with Rex three quarters of the way down the line of heavily laden animals, 'We've got to be careful here boss,' Ranjit called back to Rex.

When Rex arrived at the spot indicated by Ranjit, his heart missed a beat at the sight of a narrow ledge, below which lay a drop of several 100 feet. Slowly and carefully, the two men worked as a team coaxing the animals across the ledge roped together in groups of five. The nerve-wracking job was almost completed. It was with only 10 animals to go when one of the mules put a foot over the edge, rattling the loose stones and sending a small avalanche over the cliff. This alarmed the others who then tried to gallop across the shelf.

In a kind of hideous slow motion, Rex watched helplessly as the mules fell out into space, their hooves flailing uselessly. If mules are capable of screaming, then these mules screamed as they disappeared from view. Rex felt sick, but he didn't have time to dwell on the matter as the other mules, hearing the death cries of their companions, became nervous and restive. It took Rex all his ingenuity to coax the last five over the narrow ledge.

They continued on their way shaken but glad to be alive, picking their way with even greater care. It was very late in the evening when they eventually crested the last ridge and began the long descent.

'We'll never find them in the dark,' Rex whispered to Ranjit.

'Yes, best we lie down for the night boss,' said Ranjit.

Selecting a sheltering rock, unwilling to light a fire lest it should attract unwelcome Japanese guests, they bedded down, worn out by the rigours of the day.

In the morning, Ranjit seemed to know by instinct the right direction to take. Even so, it was well past midday before they caught up with the regiment they were sent to supply. The soldiers who had retreated right up through Burma from the Rangoon area were tired gaunt men of little words. Having a victorious army is one thing, but an army on the run is quite another. It seemed to the newcomers that the soldiers were constantly looking over their shoulders, due apparently to the Japs disconcerting habit of encircling the enemy and appearing where least expected. Rex and Ranjit were treated to a good meal, then when darkness fell, they began the return trip over the range back to Assam.

The due date for the birth of the baby came and went. It almost seemed as if the infant was reluctant to face the world. Madge was desperately short of money. She could only afford to buy the bare essentials for the coming child. Until, that is, a brief very welcome visit from Reg.

He had been posted to India for a short spell. He gave his sister a bear hug and anxiously peered into her face.

'Apart from baby weight, you look as if you've lost weight, my girl,' Reg said sternly. 'That won't do you know, but I have something here to cheer you up.'

So saying he picked a parcel from his suitcase.

'For me?' Madge inquired with a little smile.

She unwrapped the parcel and gazed at a beautiful carving of the Madonna.

'It was carved from an elephant's tusk,' Reg explained, holding it up to show the marks on the bottom of the statue.

'It's lovely, Reg. I'll always treasure it. Thank you so much.'

She kissed her brother. Reg was silent as he looked at the pathetic bundle of tiny clothes and nappies laid out for the new arrival.

'Mum told me that Rex hasn't sent any money for the baby.'

Madge's eyes filled with tears.

'Well, this might just tide you over for a bit,' Reg held out a small roll of notes.

'Oh, no, Reg, you've been more than generous. I just can't take any more money from you.'

'It's not for you, silly girl. It's for my little nephew or niece.'

He was rewarded with a watery smile from Madge.

After a few days, Reg asked Madge to explain as much as she could about Rex's highland family. He listened carefully and his reaction was scornful, 'I've never heard so much rubbish in my life, and to prove it to you, I'm going up to Carnegie library in Dunfermline to look up the Scottish version of *Who's Who*.'

Several hours later, Reg returned and had to apologise to his sister. Apparently, everything Rex had told her was true.

Madge sat hunched over the living room chair in her parents' house, tears streaming down her face, 'What on earth is the matter?' Lilian asked her daughter, 'I've just had a letter from Rex. He's cancelled the last cheque he sent. I haven't had any money for ages, the baby will need all sorts of baby things and you and Dad need some rent. You can't keep me for nothing forever!' Madge raised her streaming face to her mother.

'You leave it to me,' Lilian said stoutly.

Within a week, Madge got another letter containing a welcome cheque. Her eyes shining, she went to her mother, 'What did you say to him, Mum? He sent a cheque!'

'You don't think for one minute I wrote to him, do you? Not likely, I wrote to his commanding officer saying that I realise it's Captain Macdonald's choice whether or not he supports his wife, but it's his duty as an officer and a gentleman to support his child.'

Apparently, the money came every month for as long Rex's Army career lasted, principally because it was deducted before he was paid.

After the baby Diane was born, Madge's health continued to deteriorate. Just before the baby's second birthday, Lilian swept briskly into the living room and announced that she going to accompany Madge to see Dr Curry, their family doctor, to see once and for all if there was anything radically wrong. Feeling too weak to argue with her mother, Madge meekly went to get her coat, and together, they sallied forth.

Dr Curry was an enormous mountain of a man. He sat in his chair thoughtfully regarding the two women over his steepled fingers. He had known Lilian since she first came to live in Scotland, and many feisty arguments they had had together.

Madge, on the other hand, was one of Dr Curry's favourite patients, uncomplaining, ready to flash a brilliant smile at one of his artful sallies, if only he was 20 years younger. But, this time, there was little time for levity. The doctor was sure that there was something seriously wrong with Madge. He didn't like the sound of her symptoms one little bit.

'I'm afraid you'll have to go to the Infirmary in Edinburgh, Marjorie. I think you need some more tests and specialist treatment. I cannot give you a diagnosis here and now because I think you might be suffering from more than one condition.'

'I understand,' Madge said quietly, 'If you give me a letter of introduction, then we'll go together,' she indicated to her mother.

Dr Curry shook hands with both women and heaving his enormous bulk from behind the desk, he escorted them to the door. Afterwards, he sat for a long moment staring into space, then sighing heavily, he punched the bell to summon the next patient.

The City Hospital

Lilian and Madge sat together on the hard wooden benches of the City Hospital. It had taken quite a few hours to reach the hospital, from Fife to Edinburgh by train, followed by a long bus journey, to finally arrive in this large gloomy room crowded with fellow visitors and patients. Bored children played, running around the benches and filling the air with shrieks and laughter, occasionally admonished by stern adults.

Madge sat with her head tilted back, leaning against the wall, her eyes closed, her hands folded quietly in her lap oblivious to the sounds and movements around her. She was utterly exhausted. For the first time, Lilian felt faint stirrings of fear. There couldn't be anything wrong with Madge, could there? Life couldn't be so cruel. Lilian had so much to atone for, so much to compensate for. Lowering her head, Lilian closed her eyes and began to pray.

After waiting for endless hours, shifting position on the unyielding benches, listening intently as the nurse read out a list of names from her clipboard, then sinking back when their names were not called, Lilian and Madge sank into a kind of lethargy in which no conversation seemed worth the effort. So much so that when at long last Madge's name was called, they failed to respond for a few minutes. On the second call, they jumped up and made their way towards the nurse.

'May I go in with my daughter?' Lilian asked.

The nurse nodded assent and ushered them into a small room where a young doctor sat holding a letter. He indicated a chair for Madge, Lilian stood near the door watching the doctor's face intently. Before the doctor began his examination, he put a thermometer in Madge's mouth and held her wrist gently. After a moment, he removed the thermometer. On glancing at the instrument, his eyebrows shot up and he quickly shook and replaced it.

'Do you feel all right, Mrs Macdonald?' he asked. Madge nodded solemnly.

Thoughtfully, the doctor rechecked the thermometer. His examination was extremely thorough, taking about half an hour in all. His expression was impassive as he completed his notes and then he gravely regarded the two anxious faces before him.

'I think it is necessary to do further tests on you, Mrs Macdonald. There are several unanswered questions that will have to be resolved before a diagnosis can be given.'

At this juncture, he turned to his staff nurse who was hovering in the background, 'Mrs Macdonald will require immediate admittance, Staff.'

'Oh, I'm sorry doctor, I'm afraid there are no beds available at the moment. Perhaps tomorrow?' the staff nurse interjected smoothly in her best professional manner.

The doctor, with more than a trace of irritability, replied tersely, 'I don't think you understand me, Staff. This woman does not leave this hospital under any circumstances. Now do I make myself clear?'

'Yes, doctor,' came the meek reply.

Lilian and Madge exchanged amused glances. Thus, young Madge found herself ensconced in the hospital, unaware that she would never leave it again.

Instantly awake, Madge lay motionless. For a split second, she experienced the feeling of disorientation before her mind caught up with reality. Where was she? Unfamiliar noises provided no clues. It was like drifting in a vacuum. Then realisation dawned, she was in the hospital.

Lilian had gone home yesterday. By the time Madge had had a bath and settled in, taken the ridiculous amount of pills prescribed for her, avoided the curious stares from neighbouring beds, lay down and pretended to fall asleep, the act became a fact and she fell into a deep dreamless sleep.

Suddenly, the full import of her predicament hit home, and a wave of self-pity swept over her. Slowly, a tear squeezed its way through her tightly closed eyes. Perhaps if she kept her eyes closed, she wouldn't have to face the day and an uncertain future.

'Well,' said a cheerful Scottish voice, 'I see you're awake. Are you going to sit up and meet your neighbours?'

Madge opened her eyes and lay staring stonily ahead, her face a petulant mask.

'Oh my, I'd just forget it if I were you, close your eyes again. If life's that bad, there's obviously no point in getting up.'

The absurdity of her situation struck Madge and she burst out in a peal of laughter.

'That's better,' the brisk young nurse with a neat head of bright red hair grinned at her, 'I'm afraid I've got another huge bunch of pills for you to take.'

'All right,' Madge agreed, 'but can you tell me how long I'll be kept in here? I have a little girl you see, and I'll have to make some arrangements for her if it's going to be a while.'

'Sorry, honey, I'm afraid I haven't a clue how long you are going to be with us, but I'm sure the doctor will be able to put your mind at rest.'

Those first few days in the hospital were the greatest test of moral courage that Madge had ever had to face in her short life. She was busy making plans with Lilian for little Diane's visits when they were interrupted by a grave-faced young doctor. He indicated that he had something private to say but Madge had a premonition that it was bad news so asked if her mother could stay. Nodding assent the young man told them both that Madge was actually suffering from two diseases. She had apparently been ill for some with tuberculosis, and unfortunately, she had developed diabetes sometime in the recent past.

'Can she be cured?' Lilian blurted out.

'I'm afraid not,' the young doctor said. 'The best we can do is keep diabetes in check, and hopefully, the tuberculosis will not develop further.'

When he had gone, Lilian returned to the subject of Diane. She was chatting away in an optimistic tone about the little one being the best thing to help Madge on the road to recovery when she caught sight of Madge's expression. She was as white as a sheet. Her face could best be described as stricken.

'What's the matter, love?' Lilian asked.

'Mum, I've got tuberculosis, don't you understand? Diane will never be allowed to come and see me in here because there is a risk that she might catch the disease.'

Lilian sat with her mouth open, 'Are you absolutely sure?'

'I've nursed on a chronic tubercular ward. That's probably where I picked this up. I know exactly what I'm talking about. Oh, my baby, oh my baby!'

Madge buried her head in her hands and wept silently, her shoulders shaking with suppressed sobs. For once, the resourceful Lilian was at a loss.

For several days following that momentous discovery, Madge wept bitterly into her pillow at night, battling with the realisation that it might be months, years even, before she could be permitted to cuddle her child again, and if God forbid, the unthinkable happened there was always the feeling that she had not said goodbye.

But hope dies hard. On the doctor's next visit, Madge was ready with her questions about Diane. Gravely, the doctor surveyed his young patient, sitting with her hands folded in her lap, the sheets tucked tightly in without a wrinkle, her dark hair neatly brushed. The tell-tale signs of her illness bright spots of colour on her cheeks, startling in her otherwise pale complexion.

'You're in the nursing profession so I understand?' he asked.

Madge nodded, and the young man smiled faintly, 'Then there's no use in my trying to pull the wool over your eyes, is there? To tell you the truth, until we do more tests, we really have no clear idea of just how advanced your tubercular condition has grown. Hopefully, with rest and the right diet, we'll be able to build you up enough to send you home. So it's up to you young lady.'

'But what about my little girl, Doctor? She's only two. Is there any way I can to see her?'

The doctor pursed his lips, 'I'm afraid the risk of infection is too great, Mrs Macdonald. I cannot agree to visits under any circumstances until we get your condition under control.'

He tried to soften the blow as Madge's face visibly fell.

'Who knows, perhaps the picture is not all doom and gloom. We might get you on your feet earlier than we anticipate.'

Lilian and Harry were sitting comfortably in front of the fire discussing the subject of Madge and how to resolve the visiting problem. Two weeks had now passed since Madge had been taken into the City Hospital. Lilian made the journey twice a week and Harry made the trip at weekends leaving Diane with Lilian's great friend Elsie until the visiting rights had been settled. The financial aspect was proving a strain; Edinburgh was a full hour away from Rosyth by connecting bus and train not including the bus trip to the City Hospital. Lilian suggested that she and Diane should move in with friends of theirs, Pat and John Brakes, who lived not far from the City Hospital in Edinburgh. As Lilian pointed out, 'They've very kindly offered to put us up. We can arrange for Madge to see Diane somehow. It will be easier from over here. Then you can come over at weekends and stay overnight.'

Both Harry and Lilian studiously avoided the subject of when Madge would be coming home although they were both certain in their own minds that Madge would pull through all right. Somehow, it seemed to tempt fate to discuss the possibilities.

Once the question of accommodation had been resolved, Lilian lapsed into silence. She had spent a great deal of time in her daughter's company of late, but strangely enough, they had not grown any closer. Lilian had made tentative gestures of affection, but although Madge never openly rebuffed her mother, nevertheless, Lilian felt that she was politely being kept at arms' length.

Brenda

Madge's face lit up when she saw her young sister swinging down the ward to greet her. Brenda's visits, though rare, were a joy. Her thick dark hair was capped by her smart WAAF cap. Her neat figure emphasised by her trim WAAF uniform. Brenda had been in the Women's Royal Air Force for two years, most of that time being spent in the north of Scotland, but an extended period of leave had brought her to visit her sister in the hospital.

Madge was eager to hear all about her sister's life in the Forces. Although they had exchanged letters, it was the sheer enthusiasm and joie de vivre that Madge craved. Holding Brenda's hands, Madge listened breathlessly to Brenda's account of her life in the WAAF.

'It has been a difficult year,' Brenda began, 'I looked at all the courses on offer and I decided that I wanted to be an instrument fitter. One of my pals decided to do it with me, so we registered. Of course, we realised that we were the only women on the course, but when the day came for us to enrol, she decided to chicken out. I was determined to see it through.'

'Good for you,' Madge enthused, 'what happened next?'

'Well, I really enjoyed the course. The boys were ever so supportive. I never felt that I couldn't handle it, but when the exams at the end of the course came up, I was especially nervous.'

Madge squeezed Brenda's hand, 'It started early in the morning. Each of the lads went in for an interview lasting approximately half an hour, but when I went in half an hour before lunch, I was asked if I would return after lunch. The lads were furious on my behalf,' Madge clucked sympathetically, 'but I said I didn't mind and the long and short of it was that I passed with very good results.'

'Then you got posted to Lossiemouth?' Madge added.

'Yes,' Brenda said, 'that was a surprise, but it's a lovely part of the country, so I didn't really mind. What I did mind was the attitude of my section leader. He is of the old school and doesn't believe he should have women in his section, so every rotten job that no one else wanted to do he gave to me. I was tempted to challenge him many times, but I just kept my mouth shut and did everything he asked of me. It seemed to me to be the only way to prove my worth.'

'Is he still being cruel to you?' Madge asked.

'Well that's the funny thing,' said Brenda, 'just recently, I felt really unwell. I had stomach cramps and a thumping headache. In fact, I felt sick, but I daren't not turn up for duty. I thought he might put me on a charge. So I was sitting at my bench when I felt the section leader's hand on my shoulders, and my heart sank. I just couldn't face even the most ordinary task.'

'Then, to my amazement, he said, "I don't think my best instrument fitter is too well this morning. I think she should go home to bed and report for duty when she feels better."'

'How about that then? That's quite enough about me. Now tell all about yourself. Mum doesn't say much as you know.'

The girls smiled at each other ruefully.

Abandoned Hope

The ward was ready. All the occupants sat expectantly. Their bedclothes completely wrinkle-free. Every face was scrubbed. Everyone's hair brushed. It was time for the all-hallowed doctor's rounds. At precisely 10 o'clock, the ward door swung inwards and the doctor entered flanked by matron and the senior staff nurse, preceding several young students, their notebooks at the ready.

Madge sat motionless in bed, her hands folded neatly in front of her. This visit simply served as a slight diversion in a long boring day. The procedure was unvaried. The doctor greeted the patients, consulted the notes, deferred to the matron, then had a few words with the students grouped at the end of each bed. Madge watched with disinterested eyes as the familiar huddle gathered together at the foot of her bed, she listened listlessly as a few words drifted over to her ears: "Pulmonary, metellis, six months".

Madge's lethargy vanished as her consciousness wrested with the concept of that "six months". What did that mean? Did it mean the unthinkable that they were discussing her life span? Suddenly, Madge felt angry with herself. She had nursed on a TB word for goodness' sake. She should have known the progress of her disease. It all fell into place, looking back she could make sense of her illness and its slow steady decline.

As she laid grappling with the enormity of the idea, another even more horrendous thought flashed into her mind. Although she was aware that visiting rights for little Diane was strictly forbidden, somewhere in the back of her mind, Madge had nurtured a very real hope that one day, she would be well enough to hold her baby in her arms and tell her how much she loved and missed her.

Just to feel that small body in her arms, to smell the baby smell, to bury her face in the little girl's neck, to stroke that impossibly silky skin. But this devastating news put paid to that hope and that was the worst thing of all to bear. Weakness overcame her and Madge laid her head back and allowed the silent tears to stream down her cheeks.

By the time, Lilian arrived at 3:00 pm. Madge had had time to pull herself together. After all, there was much to discuss. Dead on time, Lilian bustled in with fruit and clean nightclothes. Before she could utter a word, Madge leaned over and took her mother firmly by the arm. In a gesture totally out of character, she pulled her mother closer.

'Mum,' she said urgently, 'I want you to put my affairs in order because I am going to die in six months' time.'

Lilian was quick to reply, 'I've never heard such nonsense, Madge. What on earth gave you that idea?'

'I overheard the doctor discussing my case, Mum, and I realised that he was right,' Madge was pleading for her mother's understanding.

'This is utter nonsense. I refuse to believe it; I'm going to see matron,' Lilian's face was set in determined lines as she set off to find the matron.

Madge watched her mother's return, the expression on Lilian's face confirming everything that Madge had surmised. Lilian looked like an old lady as she approached the bed, defeat in every movement. For a long time, Lilian stood looking at this daughter to whom she had never felt close and to whom she had been so unfair, what cruel stroke of fate had befallen this one child to whom she had never bonded. But there was no time to dwell on the past.

Madge was eager to secure some sort of future for her small daughter, 'I am asking you and Dad to look after Diane when I am gone. She's a good little girl, please, Mum?'

'Of course,' Lilian was quick to reassure Madge, 'we'll do all we can.'

'Mum, I've been thinking about Rex more and more just lately. I feel so angry that he has just ignored us, especially Diane. She's done him no harm.'

Madge leaned over to try to put her point over more succinctly, 'I feel I have a huge burden of anger building up inside me. I can't bear the thought of dying with the bitterness still unresolved. Can you understand that, Mum? I'm going to write to Rex and tell him exactly how I feel.'

'I don't think that is a very good idea,' Lilian cautioned, 'what if he finds a way to stop Diane's maintenance? I know he has been a bad father, but think carefully before you send anything.'

For a long time, Madge sat lost in thought after her mother left. Then slowly, painfully, she drew the writing pad toward her and poised the pen over the white blank page.

Rex,

I cannot keep my feelings back any longer; it is simply beyond me to understand why you have been so cruel to our little girl and me. I know my departure from London was unfortunate but you could have made alternative arrangements for us long before Reg had to step in. I know you are a drunkard, but for once in your life, you could have stopped to think of others.

I'm dying Rex. That much is clear. I don't think it will be much longer now. My only concern is with the future of Diane. Have you given any thought to your responsibilities to the child? You didn't do very well by your first child. Will you do any better by Diane? I doubt it. I don't think you are capable of conducting a responsible adult relationship.

Nothing I have learned about you so far has led me to think so. So have asked my parents to take care of the little one after I'm gone. Why, on God's earth, why did you ask me to marry you, Rex? Nothing I ever said or did was right in your eyes: It seemed to me that you hated me. So listen to me, Rex Macdonald, I hate you. I wish I had never met you, and if it were in my power, I would wish your soul to rot in hell.

Madge.

Tired and nauseous Madge lay back on the pillows, falling almost instantly into a deep dreamless sleep. So fast asleep was she, that the ward was well into its daytime routine before Madge awoke.

Reg met Rosie at the main gate of the City Hospital; she had travelled up from her native Yorkshire to see her old friend. As they approached the ward, Reg excused himself for a moment in order to have a few words with the senior staff nurse. Rosie pushed the ward doors open and entered the large 20-bedded room, heads turned expectantly and hopefully at her entrance. Feeling self-conscious, although she was a nurse herself, Rosie walked up the ward trying not to stare too intently at each occupant.

Most of the patients were painfully thin with small patches of colour on their cheeks. As Rosie reached the end of the ward, she realised that she must have walked past Madge. Reg called her from the other end of the ward and with a burning face, Rosie returned to face her friend.

In honour of Rosie's visit, Madge was sitting up in bed. Her freshly washed hair fluffed up around her head. A fellow patient had made up her face to try to give her a healthy glow, but in fact, the result had rather the opposite effect. The make-up bordered on the grotesque; if it hadn't been so tragic it would have been comic. The two girls exchanged warm hugs and to Rosie's eternal credit and Reg's silent gratitude, Rosie never so much as batted an eyelid, although she must have been shocked by Madge's appearance.

The permitted hour passed in a flash. The three young people with so much in common laughed and chatted easily. Madge, starved of outside influences was full of questions about Rosie's nursing life. All too soon the intrusive bell clanged, signalling the end of visiting time.

With a flurry of promises to write and hopes that Madge didn't intend to outstay her welcome at the hospital, Rosie and Reg passed out of the swing doors, pausing to blow kisses and giving cheerful waves. The ward fell silent, but Madge would have been very distressed if she could have witnessed the little scenario being played out in the corridor just outside the ward.

Reg and Rosie walked silently together down the long dingy corridor, each lost in their own thoughts when suddenly, Rosie turned abruptly to face the wall. Her fist pressed tightly against her mouth, struggling for composure. It was quite a few moments before she was able to say, 'I didn't realise, oh my god I didn't realise. I just can't believe she is so brave.'

Reg put his arm around her and led her gently away, 'I'm so proud of you, Rosie. Madge is super sensitive and could pick up on any bad reactions but you put on a brave front. Now perhaps we can go and meet my mum and have a much-needed cup of tea.'

Madge had become visibly weaker, barely able to raise a tremulous smile as Lilian and Harry approached her bed. Any conversation seemed to exhaust her, but she was eager to hear any snippets of information about young Diane. She grew excited when she was told that the little girl would be appearing on the ward at any moment, her pale hands plucking at the bedclothes.

'There she is,' Lilian pointed.

'Where? I can't see her.'

Madge strained upwards searching to see beyond the tall hospital windows.

'Can you lift me up, Dad?' Madge appealed to Harry.

Harry stepped forward and gathered his beloved Madge in his arms, appalled at how light she had become and afraid to hurt her. Again Madge scanned the gardens, then turning her grey eyes to her father she broke his heart by saying in a sad voice, 'No, it's no use. I can't see my baby, but do you think she can see me?'

'I know she can,' Harry said stoutly, 'she is waving right at you, love.'

'What is she wearing?' Madge asked eagerly.

Harry silently deferred to Lilian who stepped forward and said, 'She is wearing her little blue coat and matching bonnet.'

'And the blue leggings?' Madge asked.

'Yes, she is wearing the blue leggings and she looks a real picture.'

'Is she with Evelyn?'

'Yes, Evelyn is very good with her,' Lilian assured, 'I think they are going now.'

Harry settled Madge back into her pillows. She lay utterly exhausted; her pinched face the same colour as the hospital linen. Harry felt an ominous foreboding. Lilian and Harry spent the rest of the visiting time sitting holding Madge's hand and murmuring heartening, encouraging words when she rallied occasionally. The bell signifying the end of visiting time tolled like a knell of doom which seemed to galvanise Madge into action; stretching out her hands she grasped the sleeves of both her parents, 'Please don't go, please don't go,' she whispered urgently. 'They die alone in here. They die alone and I don't want to die alone, please, Mum, Dad, please.' Tears coursed down Madge's wasted cheeks with the intensity of her appeal.

Deeply distressed and affected by this plea both Lily and Harry went to plead with the matron for the chance to stay a little bit longer

'I'm sorry,' the matron spread her hands with a gesture of finality, 'Hospitals have to have rules and that is one we can't break under any circumstances.'

Deflated they returned to Madge and with promises to come as soon as visiting hours allowed, they were shepherded out of the ward by impatient staff. The last glimpse of Madge would haunt them both forever. She was waving weakly in the direction she thought they were standing; waving to parents she could no longer see.

Epilogue

It was 5 o'clock in the morning; dawn was just beginning to paint the sky when the call came. Woken from a light fitful sleep Harry hurried down the stairs to answer the loud hammering on the door, anxious to stop the noise before the whole house was woken up.

Two Policemen waited on the doorstep and before Harry could speak the elder of the two stepped forward and asked if he was speaking to Mr Miles. When Harry nodded assent the policeman solemnly intoned that, Mrs Marjorie Macdonald had passed away at 1:30 am in the City Hospital. Mumbling his thanks Harry closed the door and made his way back upstairs to tell Lilian.

Unsure how to proceed, Lilian and Harry drifted towards the hospital as soon as it became light. They called in to see the hospital chaplain and to their surprise he offered to allow them to have some time with Madge to make their farewells. Harry gasped when she saw Madge's still, pale form lying on the bed, the sheet covering her hardly raising a bump, so thin had she become.

Lilian stared unflinchingly at her daughter and felt nothing. After a long moment, almost in a dream she wandered over towards the bed and picked up Madge's white, lifeless, almost translucent hand and stood gazing unseeingly at the tracing of blue veins and perfect filbert nails.

I should feel something, shouldn't I? Lilian's thoughts ran round and round in her head.

Madge is dead. I will never see her again. She is gone forever. Nothing would penetrate the dead feeling. Carefully replacing Madge's hand, Lilian looked at Harry who sat lost in misery, his head hanging down almost to his knees.

'Come on, Harry, it's no good staying here. We can't help her now.'

As they left the hospital ward, the matron hurried out of her office to have a word with them, 'Oh, Mr and Mrs Miles, I'm so glad that I caught you; we have to discuss the funeral arrangements. Most of our deceased patients are cremated, you know, because we are after all an isolation hospital. But we just need you to sign our consent form.'

Lilian glanced at Harry; he simply nodded and followed the matron into her office.

'What do you do with the ashes?' Harry asked.

'We put them round the rose bushes in the gardens of the hospital,' the matron replied.

'That will be fine,' Lilian said shortly.

Later that day, Lilian and Harry stood gazing out of the window of their friends' house. They were watching three-year-old Diane sitting on the garden swing swaying to and fro, scuffing the toes of her brand new shoes, lost in thought.

'Well now, what are we going to do about Diane?' Harry asked.

'Well, what do you expect me to do?' Lilian snapped defensively.

'I think we should do what we promised Madge and take her home with us to Fife,' Harry replied calmly.

'I'm just not doing it,' Lilian said angrily, 'I refuse to spend the rest of my life looking after kids. I've done my bit. Besides we know nothing about her father. What if the child turns out to be a wrong un, what then?'

'But she's only a baby, she's only three years old, besides the child is not to blame for her father,' Harry pleaded.

'I don't care, I've had enough of bloody kids, do what you like with her, she can go into a home for all I care, just don't expect me to take her home with us. I'm NOT going to take her home and that is final.' Still seething Lilian decided to take the child for a walk to clear her head. Opening the casement doors she called out to the little girl who responded immediately to her grandmother's terse command.

'Diane, come here and get your coat on. We are going for a walk.'

Hardly aware of the direction and not much caring, Lilian and Diane set off at a brisk pace, the little girl trotting to match her grandmother's longer strides. Full of bitter resentment at being forced into a situation she had never asked for, Lilian strode sightlessly along dragging the little girl behind her. Diane was aware that her Nannie was upset so she just tried hard to keep up with her. Then, just as the little girl felt as if she couldn't take another step, an astonishing thing happened. Suddenly, the child began to jump up and down, 'It's Mummy's window! It's Mummy's window. Can you lift me up, Nannie? I want to see!'

Coming to herself with a start Lilian realised that unconsciously they had walked to the wall surrounding the isolation hospital where Diane had paraded every Sunday so that Madge could wave to her child. Lilian lifted her eyes to gaze across the hospital gardens to the tall window where Madge had lain propped up waving eagerly to the little girl, blowing kisses, making loving gestures, now the empty window stared sightlessly back. Then to the alarm and consternation of the child, Lilian slid slowly down the wall and covering her face with her hands she began to sob, great gasping sobs that shook her whole frame, desperate sounds of animal anguish.

She cried for the plump baby with bewildered eyes. She cried for the punished child struggling not to cry. She cried for the broken young woman who came home to hostility. She cried for the fragile pale corpse with the perfect nails. She cried as she had never cried in her life before. Gradually Lilian became aware of a pair of little arms around her neck as the child, frightened by such a display of primitive grief, tried to comfort her Nannie. Attracted by the noise a small crowd of concerned adults had gathered and stood uncertain how to proceed, one of the women bent and timidly touched Lilian on the shoulder.

'Are you all right, dear?'

Lilian started as if she had been stung. She stood, squared her shoulders and taking young Diane by the hand, said briskly, 'Come on baby, we have some packing to do, we are going home. You, me and grandpa.'

Rex was busy exercising his mules. He had been out on the hills since early morning. His helpers were native Indians whose English was strictly limited so it was a fairly lonely existence. The mules were no substitute for human company.

Curiously, Rex was watching a small speck on the plain below riding at a fair lick towards the hills in which Rex was billeted. It was obviously nothing to do with him, Rex thought, no one would ever ride like that to see him. So where was he going? As the rider reached the foothills he was forced to dodge in a zigzag pattern to avoid the largest rocks and loose scree. Then the climb began in earnest.

Rex moved to the edge of his vantage point to keep the rider in view. Whoever he was, he was a skilled rider and as he approached Rex was able to identify him as an army scout. For the first time, the thought crossed Rex's mind that he might indeed be the scout's objective, but why? The answer dawned as the scout on his sweating, heaving, mount leaned over and queried, 'Captain Macdonald?' Rex nodded assent, upon which he was handed a small black-bordered telegram. Almost with a sense of disbelief Rex opened the small envelope and read the stark contents:

'Madge died Sunday evening. Await instructions. Lilian Miles.'

Rex stood silently.

'Excuse me, sir,' the scout recalled Rex to the present. 'is there any answer, sir?'

'No answer,' Rex said, 'I never did have an answer.'

'Sir?'

'Nothing, sergeant, there is no answer.'

Much later, Rex sat in his quarters. It was the early hours of the morning. The camp was almost silent. Rex cursed roundly as he tore yet another sheet from his notebook and threw it into the wastebasket to join dozens of its companions. It was proving to be the most difficult letter Rex had ever written in his life.

Madge's parents, what did they want to hear? An abject apology? A sympathetic dialogue? An easy answer for the child? What in God's name did one write to people one had never met, but who probably thought that he had contributed to their daughter's death? Sighing deeply Rex reflected on the irony of having two motherless daughters and being unable to look after either of them. Perhaps he'd be able to write to Madge's parents tomorrow; meanwhile, a couple of drinks wouldn't go amiss.

In 1946, Rex left India and went to join the Greek army in Serres, Macedonia. His letters cover this period in his life. His army career ended in Hong Kong in 1951, coincidently that was the year his father Reginald James Macdonald died.

Home

Moodily Rex stared out at the flying landscape. Why did the thought of returning to the land of his fathers' weigh so heavily on his mind? He was returning to Scotland to attend his father's funeral. It was a visit Rex viewed with dread. He was well aware that his entire family disapproved of him, some even viewed him with distaste, none more so than Mary, his sister to whom appearances were everything.

The funeral would be a real Scottish affair too, all doom and gloom. Sighing deeply Rex returned to his book, then after a fairly long delay the train drew out of Waverley Station heading for Inverness where his mother and father had lived. Since his mother's illness, they had both moved in with Mary, so Mary had probably added martyrdom to her repertoire Rex thought sourly. As the train pulled into the station and Rex alighted on the platform, he saw his brother-in-law Ken waiting. As Rex approached, he noticed that Ken's expression could best be described as horrified.

'What's up old chap?' Rex said breezily.

'Well, I hope you've brought a black suit,' Ken said eyeing Rex's pale cream jacket, brown flannels and bright yellow tie.

'No can do; sorry, old boy,' Rex replied, 'I haven't got a suit. I'm afraid this will have to do.'

Ken subsided with shrug, previous experience with Rex had told him that pursuing the matter further would only result in a rise in Ken's blood without changing the situation in the slightest.

They drove up to the imposing family home on the outskirts of Inverness. Mary was waiting to greet her brother. Her expression tightened as she took in Rex's outfit.

'What on earth have you got on? This is a funeral you've come to not a day out. I don't suppose for a minute you've got a decent suit to put on? Well, you can fit one of Ken's on, anything is better than that!'

Rex followed his sister into the house murmuring sarcastically under his breath.

'How nice to see you, Rex. I'm delighted you managed to come.'

Mary swung around.

'Pardon?' she snapped.

'Nothing,' Rex replied hastily.

'For goodness sake, stand still, Rex!'

Mary pulled the sleeves of Ken's black suit down, trying to make the ensemble look respectable. Rex pulled the short wide trousers low onto his hips and covered the considerable gap with a black cummerbund. He stood waiting for Mary's approval. With a loud sniff, Mary swept out of the room.

The funeral turned out to be everything that Rex thought it would be, a glum service led by a hellfire and damnation preacher, glad to find any podium in a storm. Rex glanced at his mother sitting straight-backed staring into goodness knows what. She might be thinking of her married life, sadly cut short, or she might be wondering how many people would come back to the house for a bite to eat, there was no telling.

After the service, the congregation followed the hearse to the house whereupon all the ladies disappeared inside to organise the buffet, leaving the gentlemen to proceed slowly behind the hearse to the graveyard for the interment, in the manner of Scottish funerals. As the cars glided to a halt within sight of the open grave, an icy wind developed into a full-blown gale and the rain began to pour down from a leaden sky. Umbrellas and overcoats appeared as if by magic among the huddled mourners. As Rex had neither, he stood bareheaded at the graveside paying his last respects to his father.

The capricious wind buffeted the rain in all directions ensuring that Rex was completely soaked through. The minister stood four square to the elements, his long black robes flapping like an ungainly crow, his curate trying in vain to keep the rain from his master's head with a large black umbrella. It proved a source of amusement to Rex who wondered if the curate would become airborne before the almost inaudible eulogy was over. Finally, the coffin was committed to the earth and thankfully the bedraggled group of men hastened towards their waiting cars, careful not to actually break into a run.

As they all filed into the house Rex was aware that he was the object of much interest among the ladies. As it was considered bad form to laugh or even smile at funerals, it was only when Rex reached the bedroom, to which he had been banished by a fierce whisper from Mary, that he realised the implications of the nudges and twinkling eyes. He looked a sad sight. His borrowed plumage had shrunk rather badly. His bony wrists protruded from the sleeves by quite a few inches. The trousers had broken free from the concealing cummerbund, leaving a large expanse of shirt showing below the band and his yellow socks had appeared almost in their entirety below the foreshortened trousers.

Most people would have given up at this point and simply retired gracefully, but that was simply not in Rex's nature. He quickly changed into his original cream jacket and slacks, donned the yellow tie and joined the rest of the mourners at the wake. His sister Mary was rendered speechless on his reappearance; she cast her eyes to heaven and gave up. Ken tried to keep calm while Rex passed among the company eating heartily and drinking copiously.

Elizabeth's Wedding

Later in the year, the family gathered together for the wedding of Elizabeth and David. Elizabeth had grown into a slim poised elegant young lady. Her background might have destroyed a lesser mortal, but Liz had a steel core and an indestructible sense of humour essential to her survival. Her chosen husband David was in the army, a tall quiet humorous son of a clergyman, who simply adored his tiny bride. To Elizabeth, marriage was the perfect solution, bringing her freedom from Aunt Mary's stifling regime.

Originally, when Elizabeth and David got engaged, they both thought that a meeting with Rex would be a good idea. It would give Rex a chance to meet David and put his seal of approval on the engagement. All the way down in the train to London Kings Cross, Liz fretted about her father's eccentricity of dress. She hadn't seen Rex for ages. Mary informed her that he had married a nurse during the war but that she had died soon afterwards.

'We're here, darling,' David was hanging out of the train window, 'well, I don't think you have anything to worry about with your father because, whatever he's wearing, he can't look as bad as that fellow on the platform.'

David drew his head back into the carriage and looked at Liz's stricken expression.

'Oh, my god, that's him, isn't it?'

Wordlessly Liz nodded. Rex, in his loud checked jacket, checked trousers, striped socks, striped tie and checked flat cap, looked for all the world like a comedian dressed as a bookies' runner.

Luckily the family had, with a concerted effort, persuaded Rex to hire a morning suit for his part in giving Elizabeth away. So it was with pride that Elizabeth stepped out on her father's arm, a dainty thistledown figure in a full-skirted white wedding dress.

During the time my father left the army, his father died, Liz got married and he made the ill-fated trip to Jamaica, I had no knowledge of these events. On passing the 11 plus, I went to Dunfermline High School. My grandmother and Rex exchanged quite a few letters. On her side, she was asking for maintenance; on his, he reneged on a regular basis. See the following example:

Co Messrs Lloyds Bank,
6 Pall Mall,
London,
SW.
19 May 1953.

Dear Mrs Miles,

I am in receipt of your letter of 28 April. I quite understand your anxiety and am sorry that I have not written before giving you an explanation to which you are more than entitled. I have kept putting it off in the hope that "something would turn up" that would adjust the situation without having to worry you with the facts as they, unfortunately, are at this particular time.

I terminated my service in the army in the Far East in September 1951 and was very fortunate as I thought to secure a good job in Jamaica. My work was to be concerned with horses amongst which I have spent my whole life including up to the last day of my military duty when I had a pack-horse unit in Hong Kong.

I had a great deal of difficulty getting to Jamaica, owing to the hurricane of 1951, but I managed to get a passage eventually from Holland—regardless of expense. On arrival in Jamaica, I was compelled to realise there was no job there even remotely resembling the picture that had been painted for me. It was impossible to secure a passage back to England—there just were not any vacancies owing to the suspension of the banana boats.

In addition, I became sick and was compelled to enter a sanatorium for 3 months. Eventually, after six months a steerage passage was secured and paid for by some friends I had made in Jamaica. On arrival in England, I was completely without funds and could not afford to look around for suitable employment. I had to book on at once on the Labour Exchange and accept the first thing that offered and I have been since been employed as a temporary clerk grade 3 in government service at the rate of £5-19-0 per week.

All other employees on the staff are either clerical officers earning salaries of £500 a year or temporary clerks who are in receipt of pensions from their previous careers. I am in receipt of no pension from the army for, although I put in 15 years' service and was appointed to a commission on three different occasions, such service was not concurrent. The gratuity I received on terminating my service was completely written off in my disastrous venture in Jamaica. I realise, too late, that of course I should have had proper guarantees before embarking on the project but I fear I was so keen and was being pressed to make a quick decision that allowed my enthusiasm to override a restrained consideration of all the factors.

At any rate, my hasty decision combined with the previous circumstances over which I had no control here, have put me in my present unenviable position. I cannot procure a room under 30 shillings a week and the bare necessities of food, fares to my work, laundry, clothing and actual necessities in order to hold down even this pitiable job restrict me to the minimum and I would not be able to owe anything even if I had a mind to do so. However, I am determined to improve my circumstances at the earliest moment any safe proposition presents itself, but I have to step warily.

Government service, such as I am in, has the advantage that in the case of sickness one is paid for a reasonable period before discharge, whereas in private enterprise I imagine one might not receive the same treatment. Against that there is the fear of redundancy which must continue with the wholesale "cuts" periodically made in various departments. And I realise that in the world of business I have no qualifications that can hope to command a decent salary.

My time is so fully occupied, (I leave my lodgings at 7:30am and return at 6:30pm) that I have no time to search for an opening, but when my holiday becomes due I intend to devote all of it trying to improve conditions.

I have only unfolded this sorry tale as I have always realised an explanation is due to you. Will you please, believe that in no sense do I, or could I, consider my responsibilities to Diane as an irksome burden—very far from it. It is my duty and privilege to make provision to the best of my ability and I do so agree with you that she is now of an age when sound education is of paramount importance—that is why I feel particularly frustrated at being unable to cooperate fully with you.

I think you have been wonderful in your devotion and care of the little girl and it is my most earnest desire to be able to participate more generously in ensuring her a happy and carefree future. I only fear sickness or discharge but pin my faith on securing something better than the enclosed pay slips show. I will inform you at once when I am able to increase the allowance.

Sincerely yours,
Alastair Macdonald.

I think anyone reading the preceding letter would come to the conclusion that Rex Macdonald was a highly educated articulate man. However, I have no idea what my grandmother thought on receipt of this letter, the mind boggles.

My father spent the next 20 years of his life doing various fairly ordinary jobs, staying anywhere he could find, until his physical and mental health broke down. After four suicide attempts, he was taken into an asylum. There he met a sympathetic psychiatrist who, as part of his recovery programme, suggested that Rex write down the reasons he felt he had ended up in the asylum.

Control

The last human characteristic that I can highlight is parental control, that is, the control of my grandmother Lilian had over my childhood due to the unfortunate death of my mother and the defection of my father. I cannot pretend she was anything like Liz's Grannie Ogre, but she was a Victorian matriarch. Having brought up four children of her own, the thought of bringing up a young granddaughter didn't faze her at all.

The next few pages detail how my father's unusual life impacted my life. Nannie was controlling. Victorian values reigned. You do what you're told, when you're told. You eat whatever you're given. You never ever answer back. Thus, you're seen and not heard. Hugging a child was unthinkable. This is possibly why I remember, when I went to Africa to visit Uncle Don, a doctor in Zimbabwe (Northern Rhodesia), on Grandpa's pools win, I met one of Don's domestic staff, a large jolly black lady called Nanny. After my correspondence lessons, we would sit together on the banks of a stream, where I was curled up on Nanny's ample lap, my head pillowed on Nanny's large soft breasts as she quietly crooned an African lullaby.

Eendi Peendi, Eemi Wanna Mosey, Ano da, ano da.

I suppose at seven I was quite old to be cradled in such a fashion, but somehow I felt that this kind lady understood that I was starved of close maternal love, I look back with great affection to the loving friendly lady who provided it.

On the way home to Scotland, we docked in at Port Said to meet Reg and his new wife Vivienne. I think the next few sentences encapsulate my Nannie's entire view of child care. The adults stood on the corner of an amazing African market chatting about family matters.

I gazed enchanted at the market, snake charmers, stilt walkers, tightrope walkers. Suddenly, I saw something I thought Nannie must see, so I gently tweaked the hem of her dress. Of course, she ignored it. Again my gaze went to the market, no, it had to be brought to her attention. So again I tweaked her dress. Again she ignored it. Almost as if by a magnet my gaze was drawn to something I thought Nannie just must see. Greatly daring I tweaked her dress for the third time.

'Excuse me!' Nannie snapped as she whirled around. Grasping my large sun hat on each side, she rammed it down over my ears leaving just my chin visible.

'Well, that takes care of that,' she said, dusting off her hands and returning to the conversation.

What a train! The coaches were so numerous they disappeared into the distance far beyond the wooden platform at which it had stopped.

'I won't be long,' Nannie told me as she left me sitting on our mountain of cases while she and Grandpa left to sort out our tickets, luggage, seating etc. As soon as they disappeared, I had a distinct feeling of unease, what if they didn't come back, what if the train left without them, what if they couldn't find me again? Suddenly, the train lurched forward. My heart began to race, the train was going and we were all going to miss it. But no, nothing happened.

Then a shrill whistle blasted in my ear, surely that was the signal for the off? Frantically, I scanned the platform for a reassuring glimpse of Nannie and Grandpa. No sign, but again the train didn't move. A large black man in guards uniform came running up the platform waving a green flag and shouting loudly. In my fevered imagination, he was telling everyone to get on board because the train was about to leave. My bottom lip began to tremble uncontrollably. Where were they? Didn't they care that they'd miss the train? Tears began to slowly roll down my cheeks, until unable to bear the strain any longer, I began to sob in earnest.

A kind couple stopped to offer me some comfort. They, in turn, were joined by other concerned people, all murmuring about the heartlessness of people who could leave a child alone like this. All in all, there was quite a sizeable crowd gathered around me, through which Nannie had to fight. Glaring defiance at the "tutters", she hissed at me, 'How could you be so stupid? You knew we wouldn't be long!'

At last, we were all on board and the train trundled out of the station. At first, everyone stared out at the sun-baked Angolan landscape flowing before their interested gaze. However, as the journey lasted 11 days and nights through the largely empty Angolan deserts, the interest began to wane. The trip was punctuated by infrequent stops at isolated stations to refuel and restock with fresh provisions.

At the first of these stops, Nannie and Grandpa got off the train to stretch their legs, buy drinks, papers, etc., leaving me sitting on the train guarding all our personal possessions. Again the train shunted backwards and forwards, whistles blew and guards rushed back and forth before my panic-stricken eyes. This time Nannie had to fight her way along a packed corridor into the crowded carriage where I was crying inconsolably—Nannie was incandescent!

As the days progressed, the passengers began to look and feel a little worse for wear. Gritty dust settled everywhere; in their hair, on their clothes, on the food, in the bedclothes and under their nails. Not surprisingly tempers became short and arguments flared over trivial issues. So it was with a real sense of relief when the train rolled into Elizabethville and everyone disembarked to find accommodation where they could freshen up before the next stage of the journey; the viewing of the magnificent Victoria Falls. I wasn't included in the trip to the Falls. I was parked in the hotel lounge surrounded by luggage, with strict instructions from Nannie not to show her up by bursting into tears the moment her back was turned, 'BECAUSE THEY WOULDN'T BE LONG!' But the time scale to an adult is very different to a very nervous frightened child, anxiously I watched people come and go, several years passed, my bottom lip began to quiver and once again my eyes filled with tears….

I must just add an interesting letter written by a Mrs Gladys Rose about my father who spent his last years under the auspices of RUKBA, quoted verbatim.

Dear Mrs Elliott,

Firstly, may I wish you and your family a very Happy Christmas and a Prosperous New Year. Secondly, thank you for your kind letter—I must apologise for the delay in answering—but time goes so quickly.

You say that I mustn't think you were entirely callous, of course you weren't, the boot was entirely on the other foot.

I knew your father for about 10 years when he became an annuitant of the charity Royal United Kingdom Beneficent Association, RUKBA for short, so he told me a very great deal about his life from his earliest childhood. He was a character, had great charm, and was the most selfish person I have ever met. Your aunt thinks he had an unhappy life only when he ran out of money and at least he did end his life peacefully and comfortably.

The hardest time for him was when he was at Nazareth House, but they took him in when no one else would. I fear your great-grandmother thoroughly spoilt him, he had a flat in Jermyn Street, Mayfair when he was 21, fast motorcycles, then cars, he raced horses and did show jumping when it was only the army that did so. The time he enjoyed best was when he was with the Indian army in the Khyber Pass, and then Hong Kong and Greece. He came out with good gratuity but blew it all in Jamaica.

Life was tough when he came back to England—but he did get himself a job and did very well until he had an operation and was unable to work and had to live on his income, which was comfortable before the war, but very little when inflation started. Your great-grandmother, wise woman, as you know, put the money in trust for she knew he would quickly dissipate it.

The sad part I feel is that he missed out on a happy family life. Make no mistake, however, his life was of his own choosing. He loved all the good things of life and had them come what way until it was not possible. I feel he must have left a lot of heartache through his life. I'm appalled that he let your great-grandmother bring you up and then your aunt without either contributing or enquiring after your welfare.

At his special request, only a sister from Nazareth House and I went to his funeral, and I was most particular about carrying out his request. He died very happily and peacefully in his own bed, and I kept him at home until the cremation, much better than a Chapel of Rest. I was fond of your father, but recognised him for what he was. I hope you don't mind me telling you the truth but I'm afraid I think he was very naughty.

Kind regards,
Gladys Rose.

I think that Nazareth House was not ideal in Rex's opinion for somewhere to spend his remaining years. So he was lucky to hear of a lady called Mrs Gladys Rose who, with her husband, had formed a society called RUBKA. Apparently, it was to give a helping hand to professional people who had fallen on hard times. More of Mrs Rose later.

Rex belonged to a Scottish highland family and because he was the eldest (this was later challenged by a New Zealand family who had a stronger claim to the Representership, and rightly so) he inherited the title of Representer of that branch of the Macdonald clan, primogeniture it's called.

The reason for the previous sentence is because Rex got a visit from his younger sister Mary Garner-Smith just before he died. Apparently, she gave him £100 to sign away his Representership which she then had legally bestowed on her son. Perhaps not the most admirable action, but as it didn't impact anyone's life, I don't suppose it matters.

Rex died in 1981, aged 81. He left a total of £6,000 which was the amount left in his trust fund donated by his grandmother. This sum of money left a dilemma for the Public Trustee. But due to the collusion between two ladies, one in the Public Trustee Office and Mrs Rose. The following letter explains this:

'Dear Mrs Shuckard,

The "plot thickens", your letter 21 October tells me Diane was married in Scotland in 1962, and then you were "turning south of the border". What are you? The Sherlock Holmes of the Public Trustee Office? Why hasn't television discovered the exciting investigation of the Public Trustee Office? How about you starting to write?

Look what Mortimer does for the Law and Herriot for the vets, Gordon for Drs, why should you go unsung? Forgive me for getting frivolous, but I dealt with the Court of Protection for a LONG time and they are very sombre. Mind you, I did manage a tiny weeny crack once! Down to earth!

First of all, I would be only too pleased for you to put me in touch with Diane, she may telephone me, preferably after 9:00 pm as I do a lot of voluntary work and tend to get "kept" longer than expected. NOT Saturday evenings as I always visit a crippled friend. However, I would be free to come up to London after Christmas (and please don't think I'm avaricious) if she would pay my expenses, as I have been a widow 12 years and things are a little tight. This will have to be handled most diplomatically by me and I can assure you, I will present him in the best possible light.

However, if I were honest, I have never met anyone who confidently assumed that they could have their own way in everything (not with me). He left his grandmother to bring up Elizabeth, on her death, Mrs Garner-Smith carried on. He told me he had married again in the world war—but not about Diane—he may only have known later and conveniently forgotten. Never once did he either contribute or enquire about either of his daughters. Moreover not only did the Garner-Smiths look after his daughter, but they also cared for his mother and father until their deaths; meanwhile, he was leading a gay bachelor life.

If Diane is looking for any effects, he left only clothes, which I gave to RUKBA. After paying his funeral expenses of £240 (didn't I do well?) (I kept him at home—no Chapel of Rest). There was £6,471 which went also to RUKBA. After all, they had helped keep him for a good number of years. He did leave a will and I was Executrix. Frankly, if he hadn't been with me, there wouldn't have been enough money for a funeral.

Curiously enough, I do have something which was given to me and I give with pleasure to Diane, an old copy of an army magazine with an article on mules, where Capt. Macdonald was involved. He was at his best with horses, there is a photograph which gives one no idea and is flattering. So I enclose it, and hope this will help.

I am not going to tell her that he was at one time the Door Keeper to Chelsea Town Hall and eventually Hall Bearer and LIVING on a bottle of whiskey and two pints of Jersey Cream milk, plus whatever one treated him to.

My aim will be to assure Diane that her father came from a very aristocratic Highland family and that he was a Scottish eccentric, who chose to live life according to his ideas, and after all, he was also brought up by a (his statement) wild Irish aristocrat too.

He went to Wellington and this must have been disastrous for him. He had peritonitis at 16 in the days before antibiotics, and developed a bowel syndrome with, when he came to me, disastrous results, faeces up the walls and everywhere. However, you have to trust me that I will be tact personified with Diane. I am an old SRN; my late husband was a surgeon; and I work as an Hon. Sec. for RUKBA.

I do so agree that you have said that you will pass on a letter to Elizabeth. You do say that you have not mentioned Mrs Garner-Smith to her. Have you thought, IF, she, Diane, has a son, —what does that do to the Chieftain of the Macdonald's? I assume because it is the female line it is discounted—however, he, the nephew, changed HIS name to Macdonald and Capt Macdonald's daughters' children would come first.

That is not my problem, interesting isn't it? Gives you food for thought.

Kind regards,
Gladys Rose.'

It was known that Rex had two daughters and although Liz in Canada's address was known, nothing was known about the whereabouts of his second daughter. Apparently, the Public Trustee employer had tracked me through my marriage in Rosyth in 1961, but the trail went cold after that. However, because my uncle had signed the register as Wing Commander Reginald Rittey it decided that as it was an unusual surname there couldn't be that many Wing Commanders in the Air Force with that surname. Hence I was located.

So the first I knew about my father's bequest was getting a phone call from Uncle Reg to say that the Public Trustee had been in touch with him asking if he had a relation called Diane.

'Why did they want to know?' I asked.

'I would imagine it's because your father has died,' was the answer.

For a moment, I paused, not even a father one has never met is supposed to die. After proving to the Trustee that I was indeed Diane nee Macdonald, I inherited £3,000. But the best thing about this tracing was the fact that I could request the address of my half-sister Liz. Of course, they had to get Liz's permission, which was given immediately, thus leading to the significant meeting of Rex's daughters in 1987. But, first, I had an important meeting coming up with Mrs Rose in Harrods Department Store. See letter:

'11 June 1981.
Dear Diane,

I thought you would like me to confirm in writing, our meeting on Thursday 18 June, which I am greatly looking forward to. I find I can get to Harrods by 12 noon—if that is any help. You go up in the lift to the top floor, through the picture gallery and to the Georgian restaurant. There is a comfortable lounge in which to wait.

If I get there first, I will book a table in a quiet place so that we can have a good long talk. The good thing is that no one will hurry us, or put anyone else at our table. I'm grey-haired and round and will wear a darkish blue, if warm, silky dress and jacket, if chilly, a jersey dress and jacket. I wear a double row of pearls if I wear the lightweight and a single row if the other. Do you remember the giggle we had when I was describing your aunt in Scotland and you said, "Seven sets of pearls!"

I shall bring you a copy of your father's Coat of Arms passed on sideways to your cousin James. I suppose in this case females do not inherit. Shall look forward to Thursday.

Love,
Gladys Rose.'

I did indeed meet with Mrs Rose in Harrods, a delightful lady. My father was so lucky to have spent so much time with her. By the sound of most of the correspondence, I cannot think how on earth she put up with him for so long. But, for me, the most important thing was the connection with my sister Liz. The first letter I received from her is as follows:

'Dear Diane,

Thank you for your nice card. So you went to Skye, I haven't been there since I was a child but I remember it was lovely.

I think our brand of the clan also came from N&S Uist. Actually, I am rather annoyed at our Aunt Mary Garner-Smith for engineering James inheriting the line of succession and the changing of his name to Macdonald without even discussing it with us. After all, there really isn't any "Chieftainship" as ours is a cadet branch with no family seat or money.

Also, I can't see the mandatory need for a male heir when the chief of the clan McLeod was Dame Flora for about 40 years. Anyway, I think it was pretty highhanded of her, especially as she said that our father himself wished James to inherit his name. I find that hard to believe because I know for a fact that our father despised all that highland stuff and most of our family into the bargain.

I hope you won't think I'm bitter about this, but I was brought up close to Mary Garner-Smith and she has a completely different set of values than I have. I just happen to set more store on people's human values than any inherited prestige or position.

Of course, it is really interesting to find out where one's ancestors came from and I'm rather proud of the fact that on my mother's side, I have quite a list of people who helped build Canada, the first John Galt was a missionary and his sons' merchants, and eventually, Sir Alexander Galt was one of the Fathers of Confederation, he was Minster of Finance when Canada changed to the dollar and was High Commissioner to London, the first one.

David is descended from Oliver Cromwell, whom I like to think of as the first, last and only President of Britain! By the way, I sat up all night here to watch Charles and Lady Di—everyone here thinks she's a doll. It started via satellite at 1:30 in the morning and I went to bed at 5:30 am.

Love,
Liz.
Xxxxxxx'

Macdonald Clan

I was given Liz's address, which she was delighted to give, thus paving the way for me to travel to Vancouver Island to meet her and her husband, David Elliott. So, in 1987, I flew to Canada to meet a couple of the nicest people you could wish to meet, in point of fact that proved to be the death knell of my marriage. I stayed for three weeks during which I watched a marriage in progress which was very different to my own. On landing back in the UK, I told my husband that our marriage was over. Why is another story. More about Liz, David and Vancouver Island later.

Screams for Help

In my opinion, the next few sheets give as good an analysis of my father's character as anything else. They were written on the advice of a psychiatrist who worked in the asylum where Rex was incarcerated in his later years. They seem to me to be partly an excuse for his four suicide attempts and mainly a strong sense of self-pity. How much of this can be attributed to post-traumatic stress disorder I have no idea, but I feel it may have contributed.

Suicide: The Reason Why

"CAFARD" is not a grandiose, despair, nor romantic tears shed upon the grave of an unhappy life. Nor is it impotent rage biting at humiliating shackles laid on fallen greatness. "CAFARD" is the dirge of the past that neither human contact nor call to duty can destroy. It is the desperate loneliness of the creature we have tried to smother that dies so slowly and glitters against the soiled background. It is the unguarded moment that sends an artificially created life crashing round the head of the careless "ARCHITECT" who created it.

Case 1

1948. Age 49. R.A.S.C. (ex-Indian army Remount Dept.) Animal Transport. Posted 1946 to British Military Mission, Greece as Chief Instructor Mountain Transport Training Centre, Serres, Macedonia, with overall responsibility for the training schedules of all Pack Transport Units harboured from Salonika in the West to Alexandropoulos on the Turkish border in the east. I was allotted a jeep and a British driver/batman.

Not speaking one word of Greek I was fortunate in securing as interpreter, one John Marinos, a Subaltern Officer in the Greek National Army, his English was immaculate and, in common with all Greek officers I served with, he became my confidant and close friend. Occasionally, as officer, generally based in Athens, would call on the marvellous culinary arts of my cook, Madame Andaxi, were right royally entertained. Now we come to an incident which at the time did not appear to have significance but later it was produced as "evidence" in charges laid against me, but more of that later.

Serres, a town of about 30,000 inhabitants—any one of whom I will guarantee would have accorded me a warm welcome into his family circle—despite the language barrier.

Among my friends was an aged priest. One day—at least in the evening a peasant farmer came knocking on the door of the house that was my billet and in "dumb show" he conveyed to me that the "Pappas" was very ill and had requested to see me at once.

I went to the house where he lived and in the courtyard was a mass of (say) 200 people all wailing and casting their hands to heaven. They made way for me to pass through and up an outside stairway and into a small bedroom where the Pappas lay unconscious with a distortion of his features. I know nothing of medical symptoms but I reckoned that he had had a stroke. His poor forehead was burning as was his whole body.

The doctor had been summoned but had not yet arrived but John Marinos had, thank god, and realised the urgency of action. I remembered that I had a stick of menthol in my room and sent him, only a matter of 200 yards, to my billet to get it. I applied it to Pappas' fevered brow and his respiration appeared to become less laboured almost instantaneously. The Greek doctor arrived and I immediately left—grateful that I might have afforded some measure of temporary relief.

That same evening, about 9:00 pm, a crowd collected outside my billet shouting (phonetically) "Aspro Mahli Locherghost" (the white-haired captain), while this invasion was going on all the local church bells started pealing out. This I knew to be the signal that the Holy Mother's image had been sighted and might be anywhere—on the side of a house, on a hillside, anywhere. It is certainly not for me to query, criticise or endorse a centuries-old ocular phenomenon, about which I know nothing.

But the Pappas had recovered and it was attributed to my emergency camphor stick which had been accepted as "a laying on of hands". I was led back up to the old man's room and, very weakly he indicated he would like me to "tell his beads" and kiss the Holy Cross around his neck. I felt quite dreadful about the whole incident and absolutely bogus. I tried to dismiss the whole incident but I failed.

The Greeks are a highly emotional people and I was built into a sort of legendary character which was categorically absurd but unavoidable. I happened to mention this strange phenomenon to a visiting Officer of the British Mission—he did no more than return to Athens and report to the senior authority that the B.L.O. Serres was a "Grecophile" and appeared to have a sinister relationship with the "greasy Greeks" of Macedonia. I am happy and immensely proud to be called a "Grecophile". I was, I am and shall ever remain privileged to have experienced the affection and loyalty of a brave generous-hearted people.

It must have been, I suppose, nearly a year later that the insurrection of "General Markos" and his Andartes Irregular forces started infiltration from the mountainous territory of Macedonia—including the town of Serres. The Greek National Army Brigade was alerted one night to be ready to move North to drive out the brigand forces in which were now shelling Serres in some strength.

Of course I was a British Officer acting only in an advisory capacity to the G.N.A. and should have had no active role in operations. Out of the blue, an American Combat Major (the Americans had a small military mission in Greece) appeared in the Greek Brigade Barracks and introduced himself and said he was glad to have caught me before I went up the front. He was tin hatted, bristling with arms, binoculars, map—cases—the lot. He was alone so there was plenty of room in his jeep. I said 'Give me five minutes and I'll come along with you': I ran across to the armoury and drew a "Tommy" gun and some ammunition and we were away. It was only then that I realised I was wearing a Gurka's felt headgear—it was a relic of the XIV army in Burma. I am no hero it made me feel singularly vulnerable.

About 10 miles North of Serres we came upon the first Greek troops, a section of armoured vehicles. I said cheerio to the American on hearing that the pack animals had gone forward carrying ammunition to an area in the mountains to drive the Andartes out of a mountain village called Vrontou.

I cadged a lift on one of the armoured vehicles heading for that area. Like the fool I admit to being, I stood up in the turret to see what might be happening. Instantly I felt as if my head had been knocked completely off my body but I didn't feel much pain. I had been shot through the neck within a quarter inch of the jugular vein.

There was a lot of blood all over the place but a field dressing was the best that could be provided until a vehicle could be commandeered to rush me back to the Greek Military Hospital in Serres. There, having sutured the wound and put me to bed for a week they improvised a wonderful cradle which I had to wear for nearly six months.

By subterfuge and lies, we tried our best to smother the true facts of how I received the wound. But somehow the facts leaked out and I was superseded as BLO to the mountain Training Centre by a Major who had spent the entire war in Cairo and two beardless, useless 2/Lts direct from Sandhurst.

They were accompanied by a cadre of British sergeants direct from the Animal Training Centre at Aldershot.

The Greek officers were in a state of open revolt and bitterly resented the attitude and invasion by this new authoritative, yet totally ignorant of war conditions. I knew that disciplinary action was pending against myself when the evidence was completed. What did B.L.O. stand for? British Liaison Officer. How can you successfully liaise if you don't integrate as fully as possible?

I therefore decided that it was preferable to "opt out" on Greek soil where I was privileged to have the affection and respect and above all, loyalty of the people who had offered me such generous hospitality. I took the appropriate action by the misfortune that has persistently dogged me all along the line to my present circumstances. John Marinos, my trusted friend interpreter sensed that there was "something in the air" although I had not, of course, confided my solution to him, became anxious and tried my door-of course to find it locked.

He climbed the balcony and broke the window. I was rushed to the Greek Military Hospital in Serres where I was in a coma for six days. When eventually I regained consciousness, no Greek officers were permitted to visit me. I was eventually transported by stretcher to the B.M.H. at Salonika. After a few days, a "red-tabbed" British officer came to warn me that a summary of evidence would be recorded as soon as I was fit enough and there were all the elements pointing to a Court Martial for bearing arms in an affray in which British intervention was not authorised.

By the middle of the same night, I was awoken by somebody shaking my arm and there was my good friend Capt. George Fourtis, the Greek Chief Instructor from the

M.T.T.C. Serres. He had broken into the hospital in civilian clothes and had to get out again so only dared to hand me an envelope with a promise that no action would be taken against me.

The Greeks, at the highest possible level, had ensured this. The envelope contained a copy of the highest commendation in the form of a citation in an Order for the Day, signed by the Greek army commander. This is available for inspection.

In due course, I was discharged from B.M.H. Salonika with a label attached to my battledress blouse giving my name, rank and number, shipped to Port Said and put in the psychopath compound at Fayid in the Canal Zone.

I was then sent to a convalescent camp on the canal bank where I spent a very carefree three months. Then came a summons to report to the local area commander. I did so and the following conversation took place:

'Good morning, Captain Macdonald, isn't it?'

(me) 'Yes, sir.'

'Sit down; have a cigarette!'

(me) 'Thank you, sir.'

'Well, you are something of a "problem child". We have few Horse Transport Companies in the canal zone and each has an O.C. I can only suggest that, with the experience of an Ex-Remount Officer, you would be most profitably employed as an advisor in horsemanship to the companies in the area.'

(me) 'Thank you, sir. I will do my best.'

Case 2

1953. Age 54. Location: Surbiton Surrey.

Occupation: Temp clerk Grade ill Civil Service. £5 a week.

Employed at 248 M.U. RAF. Chessington, Surrey.

All the other TCs were men of 60+, in receipt of pensions from their previous employers. The wage provided by their employment at Chessington was to "help out" until they attained the age of 65 and were able to draw the state pension. When I joined, the Manager of the Labour Exchange at Kingston had advised me to apply for it as I obviously would be unable to support myself adequately with only my uncertain private income to fall back on. The only other job on his books was for a dustman at £7 per week, but obviously, this was physically and socially totally unacceptable. I, fortunately, had some friends from pre-war days living in Surbiton.

The RAF station Chessington was some four miles distant but on a bus route. I joined for duty and undertook an office boy's work—addressing envelopes and dispatching requisitions. After three months, the clerical officer in charge of the department was moved to another department and I was told to carry on his job until his replacement arrived. I must have done the job efficiently as no replacement ever showed up. My job entailed the handling of secret and confidential documents—the de-coding of cyphered telegrams—all for £5 a week when a clerical officer's rating was £750 per annum. After 12 months of this, I was tipped off by an established civil servant that I should submit a claim for "substitution pay" for handling a clerical officer class one responsibilities when I only rated temp clerk grade 111 at £5 a week.

My claim had to be endorsed by the Higher Executive Officer who was responsible for the administration of the civilian staff under his authority at 248 MU. I duly submitted my claim for his endorsement and he had to endorse it because it was based on factual evidence. I perforce was immediately relieved of my job and put on card index filing which was an appropriate task for a TC 111. While these proceedings were going on at Chessington, matters at my "home" in Surbiton were deteriorating and my hostess' husband, after 30 years of married life, had gone off with another man. As a preface to the institution of divorce proceedings, the first necessity was to get rid of the male lodger (myself).

Although there never had been or could be any form of intimate relationship between us, it was palpably obvious that I must go and immediately but where? I eventually found a tiny woodcutters' cottage halfway between Chessington and Leatherhead—there was no bus service so it necessitated a three-mile walk or cycle (if I could borrow one) to work each day. The cottage was owned by a very elderly couple and only had two bedrooms and would rent me one provided their son could share it at weekends. Above all, it had a wired enclosure with a tool shed where I could keep my beloved dogs (two whippets) that provided my only comfort in what were going to be desperately lonely and uncomfortable circumstances.

The room was booked, I recall only too painfully well on a Saturday, and I was to move in the following day—Sunday—and gave the woman £3 to include my evening high tea when I returned from work. Sunday came and with it driving wind and rain. I loaded up my belongings and my dogs and set off for my new "home". When we arrived at the cottage, there was an envelope pinned on the door simply stating: 'Decided there is no room here. Please don't call again—Deposit enclosed.' So now—what?

In those days, I did not receive any financial aid from my mother—so I was penniless and homeless for the necessity of earning £5 per week. As I saw it then and as I see it 20 years later, I had no option other than to "opt out". I had a massive supply of drugs that I had brought home with me from Jamaica and I decided on a massive overdose. My dear faithful dogs invariably slept on my bed but I felt an abhorrence against them being in the room. I locked the door and eventually partially regained sporadic consciousness to find myself in a ward in Epsom Hospital. Suicide in those days was still an indictable offence.

A couple of days later, having had to make an X on a document—I still don't know the nature of its content. I was removed—stretcher came and arrived at Brookwood Asylum—three miles from Chobham where I had spent the happiest childhood ever known in the care of my grandmother, but more of that in another statement I will provide if I am spared the time. This document is only a very poor resume of a tape recording dealing with suicide and the reasons why.

On arrival, I was taken to a padded cell (they still had them in the top security ward in those days). Stripped naked and given a blanket bath—thence clad in an institution night-shirt. Wheeled me on a trolley to the Reception Ward containing 16 patients. It was only then, on trying to get out of bed to go to the toilet that I realised I had lost all power in my legs and it was to take three months to gain control. On this Reception Ward in neighbouring cots, I had as associates—a murderer, a punch-drunk professional boxer, an individual convicted on 30 counts of indecent exposure and many more deviations and variations of mentally deranged people.

Wooden platters and wooden spoons were issued at meal times and the building was permanently locked. There was a room set aside of two hours daily for "association" but I never used it. By stealth and cunning, I managed eventually to gain access to the chargehand's office to discover that I was held under a "temp/cert". This could mean anything from a few months to a straight "cert" which meant life (remember this was 20 years ago). When I had recovered sufficiently, I declined to join any occupational therapy. I had failed in my suicide bid and I had paid this horrifying price—I owed nobody anything.

After five months, the administration sent a document for my mother's endorsement sponsoring my discharge. The form was returned blank with an annotation saying that she did not feel in a position to endorse the form as a sponsor as we had been a divided family and she had had no contact with me for many years—this was true, but it spelt ruin for me. I requested an interview with the registrar and asked him to personally sponsor my discharge. He said that such a procedure was not possible. I then informed him that if I did not receive my immediate discharge, I would devote every hour of every day to devising a means of escape. He said that was a very unwise declaration, but nevertheless, three days later, I was provided with a railway warrant to London Waterloo Station.

My Job at Chessington was still open and I had saved up about £50 in sick benefit. I travelled down to Surbiton and booked in at a sleazy private hotel to find my bearings. I found them in a small room at Chessington near the gates of 248 MU. The landlord, a retired Master At Arms R.N., this was the chance he had been waiting for all his life—to get his own back on the "officer" and by god he took it. I suffered every indignity imaginable at his hands. When I reported back at 248 MU, I was placed in the card index filing department—a soul-destroying repetitive task that any child of six or seven could fulfil adequately.

I worked in a large Nissan hut with about 20 T.C.s. All were manifestly intrigued by the re-entry into their community of this real live exhibit from the "looney bin". Damn the £5 a week and the bloody-minded bullying Master At Arms, I ran away without giving notice. I went to London and read all the postcard advertisement cards in stationers' windows and one read:

'Furnished room to let, 17 First Street, Chelsea. 25/- per week.

I was by now penniless and homeless. My mother was living at the Basil Street Hotel, Knightsbridge and I went to see her and asked her if she would go to the address advertised and pay the rent as I had no job. She agreed to inspect the place. Next day, I received a letter from her saying.

'Welcome to your new home—how lucky you are and you can make a home there for years. I could not actually see your room as I can't manage stairs but you should be very contented there as the landlady is a stout jolly Irish woman who says she will provide you with a Sunday lunch for 2/6, etc.'

I moved in. The establishment was known in the locality as "The Shamrock Hotel" as it was the "flop house" of half a dozen drunken, brawling Irish navvies who worked on building sites. It was a three-storied house with a cold water tap halfway down the stairs (I was on the top floor) and an outside WC situated in the backyard. I was to remain here for three years which brings me to Case 3.

Case 3

1954. So I am 55 years old and unemployed with a total income of just under £3 a week but only credited to my bank as and when dividends are received and my mother has temporarily guaranteed my rent at the Shamrock in the sum of 25/- weekly. I register immediately at the Labour Exchange but they have nothing on their books and hold out no hope of anything in the future. I bought the local newspaper "The West London Gazette" scanned the situations vacant and see:

'Doorman required at Chelsea Town Hall, must be of good appearance and smart. Would suit active pensioner. Apply in writing for interview enclosing recent testimonials. Town Clerks Office, Chelsea Town Hall.'

I applied for an interview with the Town Clerk and found six chairs lined up outside the TCs Office. Five were occupied and I filled the vacancy. Eventually, the first applicant was called in. His interview lasted about 10 minutes—he came out and had a hurried whispered confabulation with the others, and they all left the building without waiting as the first man disclosed that there was no overtime payable—which made the job at £5 a week totally unacceptable. Thus, as the only applicant still waiting for interview, I was taken in front to the TC. He invited me to sit down and commenced to question me about my services in the Great War and World War II and asked why after 15 years' service overall, I was not in receipt of a pension.

I explained that it was due to broken service and that I had been retired on each occasion with a gratuity. He summed up that I was perfectly suitable, and probably unique in the official nomenclature of doorman as the wages were less than received by cleaners employed under the joint Whitley Council. The pay was therefore a repetition of Chessington £5 a week.

The TC further explained that no gratuities were even proffered to government employees, so I must realise the incredible difference between the post of doorman at a public building and doorman at a West End Hotel who would be well off by anybody's standards. I explained that I was literally fighting for survival, that I was 55 years old and therefore virtually unemployable, but if I took it I would do it to the best of my ability.

I was engaged to start the following Monday. I took up my station on the main door and my territory was approximately six-foot square. My hours were 44 per week which meant eight hours for five days (Mon to Frid.) and four hours on Saturdays, standing on a fixed spot. Anyone may try for one day only, and they will realise the physical test it imposes. I was a matter of the greatest speculation amongst the staff—was I out of prison? Was I for some reason trying to smother my identity? I was suspect—of what?

Nobody knew the lowest paid member of the Town Hall staff and obviously a toff who had "opted out" or been discarded by society. I had embarked upon what I consider to have been a form of spiritual, moral and social crucifixion that was to last me for seven nightmare years. Chelsea was rapidly losing its characteristics as the artists' Mecca and was becoming the focal point of fashion.

Every day and sometimes many times a day people from Lt-Generals downwards to Subalterns and other ranks would mount the steps to do business and would halt in their travels to see a late brother officer holding open the door to direct them to their appropriate departments. All were incredulous, some discomfited and a few intensely loyal.

This period of doorman was to last three years, but had I known it, there was worse to come. I was still residing in The Shamrock Hotel on First Street and walking every day to work, stopping on the way at a café (long demolished) for a slice of dripping toast and a cup of tea and after 5:00 pm when I finished my work, I used to travel down to the "coloureds only" area around the infamous area of Cable street. Here, having mixed over the years with exclusively coloured people, I was "persona grata" within that infamous square mile, whereby I could lose an identity that was too mortifying to live with. Sometimes I had my pocket picked of the small amounts that might be in it but far more often I was given a bottle of Scotch or was a guest in the "coloureds only" cafe for a meal. I had met in Chelsea a Russian woman who was a key figure in the Guild of Guides and she was eager to sponsor me as a courier for the organisation. This entailed a six-week crash course of the tourist (mostly Americans) places of historical interest such as The Tower, Windsor Castle, Stratford-on-Avon etc. The rate of pay was £5 per day tips and I could be assured of five-day bookings every week, but it necessitated a normal social background and a good wardrobe—there was no possibility of my raising the sort of money necessary so I had to turn it down.

It must have been 1957 when quite suddenly The Shamrock Hotel was closed down and I had to move—where, for goodness sake? In Chelsea for £2 per week which my mother was by now allowing me? I eventually achieved a camp bed in a tiny room in the ground-floor flat of an ex-society tart that I had known during World War I. There I moved.

Just about this time my friend the Macebearer/Mayors' Attendant, Chelsea committed suicide from overwork and strain—so he claimed in his last deposition. I was summoned and offered the vacancy as Macebearer/Mayors' Attendant/Doorman at a remuneration of £8 per week, no overtime. I did not realise at the time that I had been properly "caught". I was employed under the Charter of National Association Local Government Officers, which is a full-time appointment, but they had added doorman, which is also a whole-time appointment sponsored under The Whitley Joint Council Charter. So, in short, they had caught me for two jobs, under different authorities, for the wages of one, but I did not realise this at the time of signing.

The tour of duty was always 12 and frequently 16 hours a day, Mayoral Receptions, visiting Neighbouring Receptions, the Trooping of the Colour, Founders Day at Chelsea Royal Hospital, opening this, closing that etc. I, by nature of my assignment, was the last person to be released. For after the ceremonies, I alone held the keys to the strong room where were deposited his chain and badge of office—having secured them, then, and only then, was I free to retire. I frequently lay on the sofa in the Mayor's parlour—too tired to walk home.

There were 55 steps from the kitchens in the basement to the Mayor's parlour and I might do this 30 times a day. One thousand six hundred fifty stairs during a working day is incredible. My Mayors were all well-disposed and kindly to me, and I enjoyed their full confidence. This triggered off violent suspicion among the other workers that I was a spy and they put me "in Coventry".

I still living in this "cubby-hole" in Upper Cheyney Row, Chelsea—God knows where I can have had meals—I can only recall one Chinese Restaurant in South Kensington where I had lunch every Sunday only. Imagine my incredible shock and surprise when I went into a small grocer's shop round the corner and saw behind the counter a box filled with stores with the address and name chalked on it: Brigadier KG.s. OBE., Red Anchor Close. He asked why I was interested and I explained that he happened to be my brother-in-law and his house was exactly opposite my house.

That night after dark, I went through the archway and there were I suppose about four delightful cottages converted to maisonettes and sitting in the front lounge was my own mother. I could not believe that my own family had crept in on my blind side and were living within 100 yards of my wretched "doss" in Upper Cheyney Row, but I could only strangle it among all the other sordid indignities that were pursuing me to an inevitable conclusion.

I had for some time, perhaps a year, been suffering from a swelling rapidly increasing to the point where my innards were prolapsing into my scrotum bag. I could not report sick as I knew the operation would obviate my ever resuming any sort of physical work and I was now nearly 60 years of age. One day, my brother-in-law called at the Town Hall to see me.

I took him down to the workers' washing-up room where there were a couple of chairs. Almost at once the Head Hall Keeper, and incidentally my only friend on the staff, appeared. I introduced him to my brother-in-law and said to him, I quote, 'Fred, would you take on my job?' He replied, 'I would sooner give up my job after 30 years and my pension than do so.' My brother-in-law left almost immediately.

Some few days later, the doorbell rang at my "doss" in Upper Cheyney Row. Expecting it to be the Mayor's chauffeur, I opened the door to a very smartly dressed woman who I reckoned to be in her 30s. She enquired for "Captain Macdonald".

'Yes,' I said.

She said, 'You don't know me, but I have been asked to call on you as I understand you are in considerable physical pain, under severe mental stress and I thought perhaps you would like to have a chat. I come from the Samaritans and the Rector suggested you might like to share your problems with us. I got my coat and took her to the pub across the road and gave her a brief outline of my many problems and we arranged that I should go to St Stephen's the next day to meet the Rector and his deputy E.R. Thus was born my association with the Samaritans—that was to remain intact for 10 years.'

'They were united that my situation and circumstances were quite untenable and must be terminated immediately. They arranged for me to go to a retreat at Pilsdon near Lyme Regis organised by a priest, Percy Smith, who had started a retreat for the rehabilitation of broken people. I arrived with all my belongings thinking it was for good, and that, having got my operation over and should it not prove fatal, I would re-join a community and not have to re-join the terrifying world of a castaway.'

Percy Smith explained that he could only accept people for rehabilitation otherwise his whole enterprise would become bogged down with the elderly and discarded. I quite understood his point and was so impressed with my very short experience there, that I got a friend of mine to get him a two-page central "Splash"—"A person with a purpose"—in the Daily Mirror. So straight back to Chelsea.

My room in Upper Cheyney Row was gone, so all I could find was a palliasse on three tea chests and a few blankets in a house that had been evacuated for demolition in Chelsea, water and light cut off but still the owner took £2 per week for rent. But still I had to be near the Town Hall on account of the late-night work and unable to afford taxis to any of the suburbs. I had to do all my washing and shaving in the Town Hall toilets and have a couple of baths in the Public Baths.

The Mayor of Chelsea at this period was a very wealthy woman and a name to conjure with in social circles. She realised how seriously ill I was and sent me to Harley Street for examination by Sir_____. He arranged for me to be admitted to King Edward VII hospital for officers. But he asked me why on god's earth I had permitted myself to deteriorate into a practically irretrievable state of disrepair. He emphasised that he could forecast no future until he had opened me up, but I must prepare to be on the sick list for an unpredictable future.

For a period of 10 days, I had to wait. The Samaritans sent me to the home of Divine Healing at Crowhurst where there was a professional staff to prepare me for hospital. I went up to stay the night prior to admission with the Mayor's chauffeur and his wife who were my very good friends. It was then that I finally made up my mind that the proposition was not valid. If I died, well I died, but were I to survive, how could I sustain my life as an invalid with no money, no home, nothing? I could not obviously bring shock and turmoil upon the chauffeur and his wife who, in good faith had befriended me.

They were out and so I left a short note on the mantelpiece enclosing a week's rent and telling them of my intentions. I, myself had no idea where the execution chamber might be—in the river? A launching onto the underground track? No, not certain enough. A hotel room—yes! That was it so I hurriedly packed a small hand case and closed the door on my life as I had known it. I had to take the normal gear for a few days away as I feared some chambermaid might undo my case to lay out my pyjamas etc. so I had to have a case for booking in at the reception. I settled for the Grosvenor Hotel, Victoria—which I had known very well before the War and knew what a solid place it was with virtually impregnable doors.

I went up, having paid my bill for one night in advance, and rang for the maid and told her I was leaving on the morrow on a long journey and would she please hang a "do not disturb" notice on the handle of my door. I observed that I only had a small tumbler suitable for cleaning my teeth, this would not contain sufficient liquid to dissolve the massive quantity of lethal tablets I proposed to swallow.

I wrote to Sir _____ the surgeon, an apology for opting out of our contract. I also wrote to the Samaritans with deep regret for so ill returning the understanding and kindness with which they had surrounded me, but not to judge me too harshly as I was in the throes and mental torture of

"CAFARD" (Please read again carefully the prologue to this statement on 173).

I had fixed the time of execution for midnight and it was by now about 9:00 pm. I wrote and posted two letters—one to my personal contact at Walbrook and one to my great supporter the Deputy Director reckoning they would receive these by the first post by which time all would be over. I did not disclose the address as I had written comprehensive instructions to facilitate the work of the police but I did give the room number. My hosts, in the meantime, had got home, read my note and immediately alerted the Samaritans and the hunt was on.

The river, the East End, the police threw a dragnet over a wide area of my known haunts. It was Eric Reid who had the brainwave, inspired by the room number (five hundred and something, I can't recall) of contacting all the West End hotels that were large enough to rate five floors. At each, he enquired if they had a visitor booked in in the name of Macdonald. The Grovenor said, 'Yes, in room 5__.'

The police were alerted and found the room locked and the "DO NOT DISTURB" notice on the door. They had not the tackle to break in and summoned the fire brigade and eventually found access to find what they concluded was a corpse as there was no recognisable respiration. However, an ambulance was sent for and I was admitted to the Intensive Care Unit at St George's Hospital, for the first time ever a new technique was tried on me (I am totally ignorant of what was done or how, so I cannot vouch for the veracity of this statement—it is what I was told).

False lungs were inserted orally and gradually and very slowly inflated and deflated to match the pulse beats. Eric remained constantly by the oxygen tent throughout the crisis days (I was unconscious for seven days) and my personal contact at Walbrook had flown to Europe before this episode—she flew straight back to London and was the first person I saw when I did regain consciousness.

I remained there for some weeks and was then discharged to the Home of Divine Healing Crowhurst into the care of Canon Bennett. I was to remain there for four months and then entered King Edward VII's Hospital for Officers, for my operation. Sir ___ the senior surgeon did his best, but of course, the years of grinding work at Chelsea had extracted a terrible physical toll and I was never to recover my health and agility—it was indeed considered a miracle that I had got away with my life, which alas, was the last thing I wished to do.

I had, of course, to tender my notice to Chelsea Town Hall and the post of Macebearer became redundant when Chelsea amalgamated with Kensington. I was now over 60 years of age and a physical wreck. I elected to take over the management of the Crowhurst Hotel. The proprietor was a Major, retired from what had also been my regiment in World War I—The Royal Horse Artillery. He had family troubles and wished to get rid of it. Being on the direct railway line from Victoria—Hastings, Crowhurst, was packed every weekend with "Chelsea-ites" sleeping three and four to a room.

As they were residents and had come specifically to see me and it was so good for the business, I had to run the bars and "chat up" the customers from 10:00 am—(maybe) 2:00am the following morning. After 12 months, I could operate no longer and had to give it up.

Where to go? I thought I would try and find a "bedsitter" in Bexhill so that I would be accessible to Canon Bennett and the Home of Divine Healing. I was directed by the Samaritans to have no direct dealings with my family at all, that they were behind me and that in them I had found a family. Indeed they lived up to their promise and my Special came down at least twice a month and we could spend a happy time, but of course, the excruciating shortage of money was always there and I was directed to apply for National Assistance, which I did and received £2 a per week. I had to report twice weekly to the Labour Exchange to draw the dole.

During the entire period, I was only offered one job (ie) a beach labourer with a sack and a stick with a sharpened ferrule picking up waste material off the beach. I demanded to see the Manager and took my credentials with me. He apologised profusely and assured me I would never receive a similar offer, I never did. When I reached the age of 65, the Social Security people came to re-assess my financial position and learned that my £3 weekly was derived from Capital Investment from a trust fund of £6,000 by the Public Trustee. It was ruled that I was indebted in the sum of £500 for benefits paid to me. They appreciated there was no intent to defraud. Therefore they were prepared to "write off" £350 leaving me to pay the balance of £150 at £1 a week. So I was £3 per week the poorer. I sought the advice of a professional Financial Adviser and provided him with all the facts and figures.

His verdict was that my financial circumstances were impossible for me to contain, and made me a personal allowance of £3 per week over a period of two years, which restored my financial equilibrium. When his most generous financial arrangement terminated at the end of the stated period, the price inflation had commenced and I was in a more precarious financial state than ever before. It was then that I decided on my only possible hope was to return to London to my original room with the chauffeur (where I had resided at the time of this third suicide attempt).

They agreed and I headed there for good. To them I was a totally different person. I no longer had the desire or the physical financial stability to be "of the company" and they came home every day to find me sitting in a dressing gown just waiting for them to come home for supper. It was, after all, their home and I apparently was introducing the elements of "an old man's home". They asked me to leave—for God's name where?

Case 4

I came back to Bexhill and left my luggage in the station waiting room while I searched for a bedsit. I went to the Bexhill West station buffet, where the landlady was a personal friend of mine, to ask her advice and while talking to her in came the same landlady where had been lodging when I left to go to Chelsea and she agreed to fix me up.

A friend of mine of 40 years' standing moved down to another room available in the same house. He, also, was down to the state of drawing National Assistance but my benefactor's allowance had expired and thus I was back to the same desperate plight as I was in two years before in a market where prices had already started to inflate.

I was in a desperate plight owing rent and vital necessities for cash. I could not carry on, nor could anyone else faced with precisely the same set of circumstances. I had to take my friend into my confidence, living in the room next door and coming in whenever he wished, I had no option. He was naturally very upset, but he agreed that my plight was intolerable and that suicide was the only certain way to terminate it. We shook hands on a secret oath that he would never disclose his knowledge of my intention. We said goodbye.

(There has been a lapse of about a week I have been feeling too ill to gather my thoughts, my eyes are nearly phased out continuing from above). My friend became uncontrollably alarmed at having conspired with me in the most final and decisive of all acts and could he be expected to live with this deadly secret for the rest of his life? No, he couldn't and I have never blamed him for breaking a promise, his nerve gave way, as mine had done. I had left instruction which I hoped would prove helpful to the police.

The day before a wardrobe dealer from Brighton had come over and given me £15 for all my possessions and clothing, leaving me with a singlet and a pair of slacks, which is all I should require for the future that lay before me. Now, of course I know nothing of what transpired over the next seven days, but apparently I was in the Intensive Care at St Helen's Hospital and then moved by ambulance to Hellingly Mental Hospital. I remember nothing of my first days there but when I did regain my awareness of my surroundings I was black and blue all over and had abrasions around my eyes and mouth. In admission, I had been assigned to the ministration of two coloured male nurses from Jamaica.

I wish to state now, categorically and without reserve, that two kinder or more considerate men never existed but apparently I was so physically violent (about which I know nothing) that had to be physically restrained for my own security. During the time I was a patient, the landlady from Bexhill came to visit me and I told her that I was approaching the Officers' Association for a grant of £50, to offset the outstanding rent arrears and provide me with sufficient money to start reequipping myself. Her reply to me was, 'Did I think she was such a heartless, mercenary bitch that she would wish to be paid for the period during which I had endured so much strain?' While in the hospital, another woman and her husband (she had been waitress in the café where I had my midday meal, seven days a week, for six years) came to see me and said that they had been very concerned over me and wanted me to make my home with them.

If I paid, I paid, if I couldn't I need not, it was as simple as that. I told them that I would come to their house as soon as I had legitimately disengaged myself from my other room. Immediately on my discharge I contacted the local Representative of the Officers' Association and he forwarded my appeal for a grant of £50 in notes. My landlady answered the door and he had ready for her the amount in rent owing, he paid it and she took it and an extra charge of £10 for damage caused by the police forcing an entry.

Remember I had not seen him yet. It was then that she let him in to see me and he told me that she had been paid and that there was a balance of £12 and he would drive me down to my new address and pay five weeks in advance. This was an utterly and completely disgraceful transaction and strictly in contravention of all the attitudes of the OA, which is entirely confidential between the Association and the officer concerned.

An O.A.P. of 84, who I have known ever since I came to Bexhill 12 years ago, a retired butler who has nothing but his savings, his pension and Social Security insisted on backing me to the extent of a loan of £50, to be repaid at £1 a week. I was thus able to a very limited extent to re-equip myself in clothing and necessities.

It was soon after arriving at my new address, a tiny bed-sitter with an electric ring and a one-bar electric heater, the cold was intense as it looked out on a small courtyard, and never got the sun, I woke up to find that my vision was fractured, no images were clearly defined. I thought nothing of it and went to Boots for Optrex and an eyebath. It didn't clear and I made an urgent appointment to see the Oculist Specialist at Bexhill Hospital.

After his preliminary examination, he diagnosed "double cataract" and when he realised it had happened instantaneously he decided I must seek advice from the Brain Specialist. By the time, I was called forward to him, I had started this abominable loss of memory. After examination, it was decided I must have suffered a haemorrhage behind the eyes. Nothing can be done. I therefore, became a prisoner for 22 hours a day, the odd two hours being devoted to crawling up the hill to Sidley to do the shopping. Somebody must have become aware of the sub-standard level I was existing on and without warning (it is all very confused), two ladies and one young man came to say that it was obvious I could no longer look after myself in such bleak circumstances and that they had secured me a vacancy in Nazareth House, they gave me 15 minutes to make up my mind.

I realised that at last after 20 years of misery, loneliness and need, I had reached the end of my journey and must forfeit my rights as a valid person. The young man called at 10:00 am the following morning and moved me bag and baggage to, what I can only equate with a petrified forest. Now turn back to page 173 CAFARD.

To Whom It May Concern

It gives me very much pleasure to testify to the general character of Mr ARW Macdonald. I have known him for several years and have been in very close contact with him in connection with civic affairs during the past four years in particular during which time I was Mayor of Chelsea for two years and deputy Mayor for two years. I have found him to be scrupulously honest, reliable, of good bearing and appearance and, at all times courteous and willing to be of assistance. My very best wishes will be with him in whatever vocation he decides to enter and I shall be happy to supply further information if called upon to do so.

Arthur J Lewis.

Is this possibly the same man?

In Conclusion

Someone whose opinion I respect made the comment that by the sound of the book, PTSD, shattered bonding and attempted suicides were all rather depressing. Thinking about it I realised that my friend was right, but I like to think that the meeting of me, my half-sister Elizabeth, her husband David, their daughter Rosemary, and son Brian, lifted the gloomy picture. Although I never met my father, I feel sorry for him. I don't remember my mother at all, but I found her story so tragic. My grandmother (Nannie) died in 1972.

Diane Catchpole, 4 March 2022.

Who Am I?

I think that back in the mists of time large clans became too unwieldy for one chief to manage, so sub-chiefs were appointed answerable to the main chief. From such an arrangement, my father was a direct descendant. The clan was the Macdonald of the Isles, and for many years the hierarchy went as follows: Lord Macdonald of the Isles, Sir Ian Macdonald of Sleat, followed by my father Alistair Reginald Macdonald of Aird and Vallay. Highland Clans use primogeniture, father to eldest son, following the male line, so my son Ross would have automatically assumed the Representership because my father only had daughters and my sister Liz had one daughter and an adopted son, who was therefore ineligible.

However, all this is irrelevant because a further change was on the horizon. A few years ago, I was informed that a man living in New Zealand had been doing research on the family, and he had discovered that our great-great-grandfathers had been brothers, and although my great-grandfather was a Canadian Senator and twice Mayor of Victoria in Vancouver Island, his great-great-grandfather was the elder and he had decamped to New Zealand many years before, thus dropping out of the family consciousness.

I met Allan Macdonald and his wife Lee when I went to New Zealand on holiday and he proved to be a splendid chap with a delightful family, but I understand that Aunt Mary never accepted his family credentials, although he had pursued the case through the High Court and won at a cost of £50,000.

So now the Clan Macdonald of the Isles reads as follows: Lord Macdonald, Sir Ian Macdonald of Sleat, Allan Macdonald, Macdonald of Vallay and Jamie Macdonald of Aird until the line becomes extinct. So my children and I are part of the Macdonald of Aird Line. As far as I know, this is as true a picture as I can paint.

Finally

Now is the time for me to say how much I enjoyed the various trips I make to Vancouver Island. I fell in love with that Island, especially Oak Bay where Liz and David lived. But most of all, I felt that I was totally accepted by Liz and David as part of their family. I even got to know Rosemary, their daughter and her family, and Brian their son and his wife. Sadly Liz lost David and moved into a Residential Home, but still I was invited to visit.

Liz's health deteriorated, but we kept up a steady correspondence until I felt that perhaps there was something amiss with Liz, so I took a flight back to Vancouver Island. Liz was then 90 years old and confined to a chair in her room. Looked after by Rosemary, whose home is in America.

I didn't really understand what Liz intended and it wasn't till I got home and received a phone call from Liz to say goodbye that I realised her intention. Liz had set in motion something called Medically Assisted Death and she died in 2018. I cannot say how much I admire her children Rosemary and Brian and their families for allowing, respecting and carrying out Liz's last wish. She had always been involved with her friends, going here and there, helping others and being independent.

But eventually, her health gave way and she ended up sitting in a chair unable even to go to the toilet without help. That, to Liz, wasn't life but an existence she didn't want. I admire her for that and I miss her forever. I wonder what Rex would have made of the warm friendship between his two daughters?

But, on the other hand, I still have a connection with Rosemary and Brian. In addition, I email Allan and Lee in New Zealand and Maryjean Onslow, Aunt Mary's elder daughter in Edinburgh. So, after many years, I feel that I am part of the Macdonald clan, of which I am justly proud.